HOW TO GET YOUR
POINT ACROSS
— IN —
30
SECONDS OR LESS

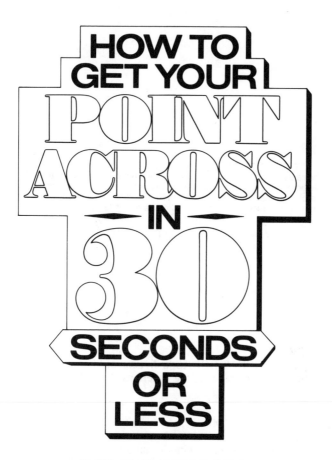

HOW TO GET YOUR POINT ACROSS IN 30 SECONDS OR LESS

MILO O. FRANK

POCKET BOOKS

New York   London   Toronto   Sydney   Singapore

POCKET BOOKS, a division of Simon & Schuster Inc.
1230 Avenue of the Americas, New York, NY 10020

Copyright © 1986 by Milo Frank

Published by arrangement with the author
Library of Congress Catalog Card Number: 85-27822

ISBN: 0-671-72752-4

First Pocket Books trade paperback printing March 1987

17   16   15   14

POCKET and colophon are registered trademarks of Simon & Schuster Inc.

Printed in the U.S.A.

To Sally with love

ACKNOWLEDGMENTS

To Terry Mayo, my most grateful appreciation for your invaluable help.

Thank you, Fred Hills, for your continuing enthusiasm and belief in this book, and to you and Burton Beals for your fine job of editing.

And thank you, Arthur and Richard Pine, for your excellent representation. Without you this book would not exist.

CONTENTS

HOW TO GET YOUR
POINT ACROSS
—IN—
30
SECONDS OR LESS

WHAT THIS BOOK WILL DO FOR YOU

Read the following aloud:

The future is a high-speed car without a driver. You have to be the driver. You have to plan. You have to decide the direction you're going to take. Do you want somebody else to make the decisions? Don't be just a passenger. Let people know what you want and where you want to go. Thirty seconds is the key. That's all the time you need to get your point across. This book will teach you how to develop and use the 30-second message in any situation. The 30-second message can put *you* in the driver's seat.

Stop!

You have just read a 30-second message.

Thirty seconds may not seem like a long time. But it's long enough to say what you want to say.

It's long enough to grab and hold your listeners' interest and attention.

It's long enough to convince or persuade your listeners.

It's long enough to make any point you want to make—and make it effectively.

It can be more valuable than three minutes, 30 minutes, or three hours.

Thirty seconds can change the direction of your career and your life.

My entire business career has been in communications of one kind or another. As a young man, I was a motion picture agent in agencies that represented many stars such as Linda Darnell, Marilyn Monroe, and Humphrey Bogart. It was my job to attract new clients, communicate and sell the talents and abilities of those we had, and negotiate the terms of their contracts. As head of talent and casting for CBS Television, I found the best actors I could for many different shows and then negotiated with *their* agents to conclude the deals. As a writer, director, and producer, I've presented the written and spoken word to a wide variety of audiences. And for years, I've been teaching practical communicating skills to business people and politicians.

I've seen careers rise and fall on the spoken word. The employee who can't communicate effectively doesn't get a raise or a promotion. The boss who can't get his point across loses the cooperation of his employees. The salesman who can't stop talking doesn't make the sale. The politician who says too little too long doesn't get reelected. They all bore us in minutes, when they could interest us in seconds.

Read the following aloud:

Communicating effectively, persuasively, and concisely can be easily learned. *How to Get Your Point Across in 30 Seconds—or Less* will show you how to get your listener's attention, keep his interest, tell a wonderful story, ask for and get what you want—all in 30 seconds. You will be able to get your point across to your business associates, your family, your friends, and all the people you deal with from the secretary to the accountant to the president of the company. Follow the simple steps outlined in this book. Use the easy techniques. You'll save time and accomplish more than you ever thought possible. And you'll have fun doing it.

Stop!

Again, you have just read a 30-second message.

Obviously, all of your business communications do not have to total 30 seconds. Building a rapport with your listener is important too. Every situation is unique. But when the time comes to make your point, make it in 30 seconds. It doesn't matter if you have five minutes or five hours to talk to your listener. The heart of the matter should take place in 30 seconds. The rest is preparation or follow-through. The right 30-second message will, in the final analysis, enable you to get your point across and keep it where it belongs—in the mind of your listener. Wherever and whenever attention is required, 30 seconds works.

When you have learned how to prepare your 30-second message, you will be able to:

- focus your thinking
- focus your writing
- focus your speaking
- keep conversations on track
- prepare any form of communication more rapidly
- be more logical and concise
- shorten interviews and meetings
- facilitate listening

- reinforce conversations and presentations
- be more effective in any interview or meeting
- use questions and answers to make your point
- heighten your confidence, and
- get better results in your business life and personal life as well.

In all the years I've been involved in the business of communicating, the single most important thing I've learned is the crucial win-or-lose value of the 30-second message.

CHAPTER One

Why 30 Seconds?

"If only he'd get to the point!"

"All right, she's got five minutes and out."

"I can't see him today. I haven't got time."

"Don't answer the phone. It might be Ellen. She talks forever."

"This is my first presentation to top management. I'd better be good and fast."

"What kind of memo is this? I haven't got time to read five pages."

"God, he talked for an hour, and I don't know what he said."

"If I get one chance to speak in the meeting, and I have to be brief, can I deliver my whole message?"

"How can I get my point across in a fifteen-minute interview?"

"They're tough businessmen. They won't listen long."

"He wants two or three minutes and that means fifteen or twenty, and it'll be a waste of time anyway."

In this hurry-hurry world, does all this sound familiar?

There are two clear and compelling reasons why 30 seconds is the ideal length of time in which to get your point across.

TIME CONSTRAINT

The first is *time constraint*—not only on yourself, but also on those you're trying to convince.

Through my film and TV work, I've seen time and tastes change; fast food, fast cars, and fast deals are commonplace today. Time waits for no man; you have to move faster just to stay even. And to move faster, you must be concise.

Do you ever think about how people judge you and about how you judge others? Your deals, jobs, money, and success can all hang on first impressions. Isn't it true that with just a few words, an image is formed in your mind and in theirs, and you and they act accordingly? Often there's only time for a few words, so they had better be the right ones. The hour of years ago is the 30 seconds of today. To survive and move ahead in business or in any other relationship, you must be able to get your point across swiftly and succinctly in 30 seconds or less.

ATTENTION SPAN

The second and more important reason why 30 seconds is the ideal length of time to get your point across is that even when a person has time to listen to you, his mind can accept only so much information in one steady flow.

How long can you or anyone pay attention to what someone is saying without letting your mind wander off to sex, money, or the other good things in life? When I ask this question, I get answers of anywhere from four hours to four seconds. One businessman in a particularly sour mood from his most recent sales meeting said zero was the attention span of his associates. That happened to be true, but only because he always talked so long and boringly that his audience turned him off before he even opened his mouth. *The attention span of the average individual is 30 seconds.*

Let me give you an example. Look around the room and concentrate on a lamp. You'll find your mind goes to something else within 30 seconds. If the lamp could move or talk, or go on and off by itself, it would recapture your attention for another 30 seconds. But without motion or change, it cannot hold you.

Think of soneone's attention span as a quarter slot machine. This machine must take in the first twenty-five cents before you can put in the second twenty-five cents. If you put in fifty cents or a dollar all at once, you'll have wasted your money and maybe even jammed the machine. It can take in only twenty-five cents at a time. Your listener can take in only 30 seconds at a time.

So if you want your listener to give up thoughts of sex and money and pay attention to you, you've got just 30 seconds. That is the attention span of the human race.

TELEVISION, RADIO, AND
THE ATTENTION SPAN

Nowhere is this better illustrated than in the field of radio and television commercials. Media research has determined 30 seconds to be the attention span of the average viewer. That's why you and I live with the 30-second attention span theory every day of our listening and viewing lives. Almost all commercials on television and radio are 30 seconds long. If those commercials didn't sell the product, whether it's a refrigerator or a politician seeking votes, the whole concept of radio and television advertising would change.

When I discuss the 30-second message with people in my communications workshops, I hear the same thing over and over again: "I can't possibly make my point in such a short time."

My answer is that television and radio do it all the time. Commercials not only grab your attention but also tell you all about the product and where and when to buy it. Here's an example of a 30-second television commercial for Galpin Ford:

"Galpin purposely bought a lot of motor homes. But all the rain kept many of our customers away. We've got too many motor homes. Buy them during our three-day sale. Save up to eighteen thousand dollars off our regular list price. The savings can pay for your vacations for years. You can take up to twelve years to pay; many have an 11.9 percent finance plan. Prices start at $16,996. See Friday's *L.A. Times* sports section. Don't wait forever. It's the things you don't do that you regret."

The result was the most successful sale of motor homes in the history of Galpin Ford, one of the largest dealers in the country. The commercial told the potential buyer what he needed to know, and all within his attention span. The important point is that a lot can be said and retained in 30 seconds. And if radio and television can do it, so can you.

THE SOUND BITE

Radio and television news also make use of the 30-second attention span. It's called the "sound bite." I asked a television news anchorwoman-reporter friend of mine, Terry Mayo, to explain to some business people just what a sound bite is, and she said:

"Because of attention span, the average time of all television news stories is one and a half minutes. The reporter needs 30 seconds to set up the story, another 30 seconds is reserved for the actuality, which means an interview or tape of what's happening, then another 30 seconds for the reporter to summarize and end the story. If I go out to interview someone about a story, I want that person to make his point in 30 seconds or less so I can pull it out and use it. That 30-second portion of the entire interview that I edit at the studio is called a 'sound bite.' If the subject doesn't make his statement in 30 seconds or less, I can't use it and it doesn't make the air."

Terry had something else to say about the 30-second rule on TV news:

"We've discovered that if you can't say it in 30 seconds, you probably can't say it at all. If you know how, you can make any point very well in 30 seconds."

An example is a moving message delivered in this dramatic and emotional television news story:

An old man had gone into the water fully clothed to save two seven-year-old children. He was still soaking wet when the television reporter interviewed him. He said, "Sure, I'm sixty-five. So what? Anybody who could swim would have gone in to save those kids, but maybe I did something else important. Maybe people should realize that when you're over sixty, you're not dead. You're productive, and retirement shouldn't be a mandatory thing."

There's a powerful message in less than 30 seconds, and the point certainly gets across. It was made by an average person under stress. It proves conclusively that you or anyone can do the same thing if you know how.

The 30-second message is always applicable, anytime and anywhere. It's a basic tool. When you master it, it'll become second nature to you. It'll create a whole new mind-set. It'll transform the way you think and deal with others every day. You'll find yourself instinctively prepared and using it all the time.

Anybody can master the art of the 30-second message by mastering a few basic principles—and these are what you are about to learn.

CHAPTER Two

Your Objective

In *The Wizard of Oz,* Dorothy had an *objective.* It was to get back home to Kansas. That's what she told the Scarecrow, the Tin Man, the Cowardly Lion, and finally the Wizard himself. She knew what she wanted. The *First Basic Principle* of the 30-second message is to have a clear-cut *objective.*

YOUR OBJECTIVE—KNOW WHAT YOU WANT

The *objective* is The Goal, The Destination, The Purpose, The End in View, The Target, The Raison d'Être. It's what you want to achieve. It's why you're there. It's what you must have in order to take effective action. It's the definitive reason for you to enter any serious business conversation or undertake any form of communication in which you have a point to make.

Here are some typical objectives in the business

19

world. Among them you may find an objective of your own.

- A man wants to get a more important job in the company where he works.
- A woman wants to open her own business.
- An assistant manager wants to take a vacation.
- A person wants to make an effective toast.
- A salesman wants to sell his product to a customer.
- An employee wants a raise.
- A manager wants to increase productivity in his department.
- A client wants to spend less for a service.
- A departmental director wants to sell an idea to management.

THE MIXED OBJECTIVE

It's surprising how often opportunity is wasted because a person has an unclear or mixed objective.

Mark Larsen, a middle manager, knows that funds are available to improve the operation of his department. He makes an appointment with the vice president in charge of budget allocations, but he's not sure what he really wants. He has a mixed objective. Here's the way the meeting goes.

MARK: I've been looking at ways to improve our productivity.
VP: Good. What are your recommendations?
MARK: Well, we could speed up our operation with a new X100 computer.

VP: But that might take us over budget. Is there an alternative?

MARK: Yes. We could hire another secretary. That would work.

VP: Which do you prefer?

MARK: I'm not sure. Maybe we should also think about an assistant—a grade above secretary.

VP: That's possible, too. What are the comparative costs?

MARK: I don't know. Let me put some figures together and get back to you.

A week later when Mark gets his figures together and goes back to the VP, it's too late. The available funds have been allocated to another department. Mark's lack of a clear-cut objective—his mixed objective—has not only cost him the help he needs but also created a poor impression in the mind of a man who is important to his future with the company.

THE SINGLE CLEAR-CUT OBJECTIVE

Here is the same interview—only this time Mark knows exactly what he wants. He has a single clear-cut objective. This is the way the interview goes.

MARK: I've been looking at ways to improve our productivity.

VP: Good. What are your recommendations?

MARK: We could speed up our operation with a new X100 computer. The rental costs are high, but it would save time and money in the long run and pay for itself in eighteen months. Here are the figures.

VP: Is there a less expensive alternative?

Mark: Yes. We could hire another secretary, or an assistant. But I don't think the end results would be the same. This is a breakdown of the comparative costs.

VP: You prefer the computer, don't you?

Mark: I do. And the manufacturer will set up the program and train us in its operation at no extra cost.

VP: Good. I'll present your figures at the next budget meeting and we'll see what we can do.

A single clear-cut objective gets Mark his computer and the recognition of management that here is a man who knows what he wants.

It's been my experience that most people in business, and even leaders in industry and government, don't really know what their objective is. Or they may choose an objective that does not best serve their interests or requirements. Only by determining your objective precisely can you take the first vital step toward getting your point across.

Here's how to determine your objective.

FINDING YOUR OBJECTIVE

Ask yourself the following questions:

Why am I going there?
What do I want to achieve?

Why do I want to have that conversation?
Why do I want to write that letter?
Why do I want to meet with this person?
Why do I want that interview?
Why do I want to address this meeting?

If two or more of your answers to these questions are the same, you have found your objective. There can be only one objective and it must be clear-cut and specific. When you have found it, give it one final check. The operative word for that check is almost always *why*. Once your objective is clear—once you know why—you can begin to prepare your message. Balance everything you plan to say against your objective. If your thoughts and words do not introduce, reinforce, or help you achieve your objective, go back to the drawing board. And when you know what your objective really is, stick to it.

THE HIDDEN OBJECTIVE

There may be times when it's bad strategy to state your objective. For example, when the Allies landed on the beaches of Normandy, they had a *hidden objective*. They made the Germans think their intention was to land elsewhere. In communications you can make this same strategy work for you.

When I was casting "Playhouse 90," one of the great live theatrical shows on television, I had a hidden objective. We wanted the best actors available, but their salaries were always more than we had in our budget. So I developed a new type of billing. It was called "guest star" billing, and I was able to convince actors to work for less than their usual salaries by describing the new "guest star" billing idea and its benefits to their careers. It was good for them as well as for us, and the hidden objective was fulfilled.

A hidden objective can work as long as *you* know what that objective is.

Every form of business communication—whether it's a job interview, a conversation between boss and employee, a memo, a presentation, a sales talk— should have a *single clear-cut objective*. Otherwise, you're wasting your time and your listeners' time. And you should know what that objective is before you open your mouth or put pen to paper.

IN 30 SECONDS—OR LESS

Your objective is your goal, purpose, or destination.

It is why you are there.

You can have only one objective.

In every form of business communication, your thoughts and words should introduce, reinforce, or help you achieve your objective.

You do not have to state your objective except to yourself.

The *First Basic Principle* of the 30-second message is to have a *single clear-cut objective*.

CHAPTER Three

Who's Listening?

Imagine you're in charge of an amphibious invasion. It's wartime. You're ready to send in the landing craft. It's midnight, pitch black. There's no moon, no stars, and there's a light, cold rain. It's time to go ashore. You don't know anything about the island, not even if it's in enemy hands. Not how many enemy troops there are, if any. Not how well armed they are, nor how fortified the island. You don't know the terrain. You don't know if you should send in one group or land in force. Should you call on covering fire? Should you bring in flamethrowers and antitank guns?

If you know nothing about what awaits you, what is or might be there, how can you know what to do? You kick yourself because all you had to do was ask your intelligence section. They had the information all the time.

Impossible? Almost. How often do you go into "unknown terrain" in the business world, not knowing who or what you're going to find when you get there? How often do you go into important meetings, make important calls, and have important conversations with your business contacts without knowing anything about them? You may very well have a clear-cut objective, but you must then select the right person for the right result, the person who can give you what you want, who can fulfill your objective, be it a job, advice, help, money, or just information. Knowing your listener and what *he* wants is the *Second Basic Principle* of the 30-second message.

THE RIGHT PERSON

One Christmas, to surprise my wife, I sent away for a luxury item, a towel warmer for our bathroom. There were two kinds offered in the catalogue, one that had to be bolted to the floor and one that stood upright without bolts. As ours is an old house, there's a marble floor and marble walls in our bathroom. Of course, I ordered the towel warmer that stood upright. It arrived just in time for Christmas, surprising my wife and me too, her with delight and me with anger, because it had to be bolted to the floor. I couldn't see myself boring holes in a marble floor.

I grabbed the Abercrombie and Fitch catalogue, got the address, and wrote a letter asking for my money back. No answer. Then I did my "select the right person for the right result" analysis. Who could give me satisfaction quickly and easily? The president of the company, of course. So I wrote him. No answer. Then I wrote again, demanding my rights. He wrote me a nice letter back saying he was looking into the matter.

No further word. I wrote again, an even tougher letter. His letter crossed mine in the mail. "Dear Mr. Frank," he wrote, "We at Abercrombie and Fitch would be glad to take the towel rack back, but you didn't buy it from us. We don't carry the item. You bought it from Hammacher Schlemmer."

I knew what my objective was—to get my money back—and I pursued it. I even chose the right person —the president of the company. But it was the wrong company.

Finally I did write the president of Hammacher Schlemmer, who was amused by the story and cheerfully refunded my money.

So once you've determined your objective, always ascertain who can give you what you want. If you're entitled to a refund on a purchase, go to the head of the company if necessary. If you want a raise, go to your boss. If a telephone operator can't help you, ask for the supervisor. If your insurance claim doesn't get taken care of, go to the senior person at your insurance company or agency.

Go to the person who can get it done.

True, sometimes you have to talk to the wrong person to get to the right person, but regardless of who you actually talk to, you should learn as many facts as you can about that person.

What exactly is the person's job or profession? What responsibilities does she have? What is his background? What are her interests or hobbies? There may be a common ground. I've found as a tennis player that if I'm dealing with a person who is or was also a tennis player, talking about tennis breaks the ice and I'm off to a good start.

Is he strong and secure in the job he holds? How much authority does she have? Is he a bureaucrat? Is she touchy about particular areas of her business? Is he shy or outgoing? Does he have a sense of humor?

Knowing who you're talking to can help guide you in planning to get what you want.

KNOW WHO YOU'RE TALKING TO

I always know precisely who I'm talking to. Here's an example.

My wife, Sally Forrest, had just gone under contract to MGM as a new young leading lady, and at the studio's request, she was attending her first big Hollywood premiere. There were cameras, mikes, floodlights, fans, and reporters, including Louella Parsons and Hedda Hopper. Sally was led up to the microphone where her boss, Dore Schary, Chief of Production for MGM, was standing. He greeted her and said some nice things about her bright future at her new home, MGM. Sally told the assemblage, over the microphone, while the cameras were rolling, how happy she was and then closed by saying to Dore Schary, "Thank you very much, Mr. Wellman." She thought he was the famous director, Bill Wellman.

As her husband, I was amused, but as her agent, I was horrified. I told Sally, in no uncertain terms, that you just do not, if you wish to succeed at the most important studio in the business, call the gentleman in charge of production, your boss, by the wrong name! She had lowered her credibility at the studio and endangered her future. I knew everybody's name and so should she!

A month or so later, Sally and I walked into a restaurant at the beach in Santa Monica, and lo and behold, sitting at a table in the corner, was the famous director, and client of the agency where I worked, Bill Wellman—the "Mr. Wellman" of Sally's mistake. By this time I had begun to see the humor in the incident, so with Sally I proceeded to his table and said, "Mr. Wellman, a month or so ago . . ." and then told him of the embarrassing but, in retrospect, funny event.

He smiled and said. "That's a very amusing story, but I'm not Bill Wellman. I'm Paul Hesse."

Paul, a famous photographer of stars, did look a bit like Bill Wellman, I told myself. So as you can see, I always know precisely who I'm talking to.

In order to get your point across in 30 seconds or less, first determine your *objective*, and second, determine the *right person* or group of persons who can give you what you want. Then learn all you can about that person or group. Finally, and most important, *know what that person or group is going to want from you.* Here's how it works.

Richard Randall, an assistant bank manager, knows the job of manager at his branch is opening up. He wants the promotion—his *objective*—and makes an appointment for an interview with the corporate executive who can give it to him—the *right person*. Then he collects all the information he can about that executive. The man

- is a workaholic
- has been in the banking business all his life
- started as a teller
- is a stickler on being polite to customers
- takes care of his employees
- likes people with ambition
- is confident and likes people who are confident
- knows all the jobs in the bank and thinks everyone there in a position of authority should also, and
- is not motivated solely by money.

Richard knows that to be persuasive and get the promotion, he must address the executive's needs and interests—not his own. He asks himself, "What does that executive want from me?" And in order to answer that question, he puts himself in the mind of the executive and thinks as the executive might. He becomes that executive. And this is what he decides the executive wants from him:

He wants some good reasons why he should give me the job.
He wants to see how much I know about the job.
He wants to know why I'd be better than other applicants.
He wants to know why I think I can do the job.
He wants to know how confident I am.
He wants to know what the job will mean to me.
He wants to know how I will get along with other employees and customers.
He wants to see how I act under the pressure of an interview.
He wants to see how I will handle questions.
He wants to know what my ambitions are.
He wants to see what kind of person I am.

He wants to see how smart I am.
He wants me to prove to him I can do the job.

Now Richard not only knows what he wants, he also knows what the executive wants from him. And that knowledge is basic to the formulation of every 30-second message. Sound complicated? Not really. By identifying with the executive who was going to interview him, Richard was able to determine the *one* thing above all others that would impress the executive favorably: his ability to do the job. So it would be up to Richard to convince the executive—in 30 seconds or less, no matter how long the interview might actually last—of just exactly that. When the time came for the interview, Richard emphasized his knowledge, his experience, his enthusiasm, and his self-confidence—in short, his ability to do the job.

There's slightly more to this scenario. Richard knew that the executive who could give him the job was primarily interested in his ability to handle it. But he also knew that the executive was crazy about softball. In fact, he was the driving force behind the bank's softball team. When the time came for the interview, Richard emphasized his knowledge, his experience, his enthusiasm, his self-confidence—and his pitching ability. All in 30 seconds or less. P.S., he got the job.

Before you begin to prepare your 30-second message, no matter what you want—a better job, a raise, a vacation, cooperation from your co-workers, a refund, a charitable contribution—you have to know who will be listening and the one thing above all others that will get a favorable reaction.

Firing at a target in the dark is not very promising. Now we have illuminated the target. You know where to aim. And you know what you want to hit. Both are essential as you prepare your ammunition—the 30-second missile.

IN 30 SECONDS—OR LESS

Go to the *right person,* the person who can give you what you want.

Know as many facts as possible about the person or persons you'll be talking to.

Identify with your listener. What does he want from you, and what one thing more than any other will get a favorable reaction from him? Knowing your listeners and what they want is the *Second Basic Principle* of the 30-second message.

CHAPTER **Four**

The Right Approach

Remember Dorothy in the Land of Oz? She and her dog Toto want to go back to Kansas. The Scarecrow wants brains. The Tin Man wants a heart. The Cowardly Lion wants courage. Those are their *objectives*. And they know the Wizard of Oz is the only person who can give them what they want. He's the *right person* to talk to. Their problem at the moment is how to get to the Emerald City to see the Wizard. They take the Yellow Brick Road. That is their *approach*.

The *Third Basic Principle* of a 30-second message is a well-formulated *approach*.

THE RIGHT APPROACH—HOW TO GET THERE

The *right approach* is the single thought or sentence that will best lead you to your objective. This thought or sentence could be referred to as the premise, root idea, concept, focus, driving force, strategy, game plan, or theme of your message. The *right approach* is also the foundation of the building, the heart of the matter, the skeleton in the body, the melody that runs through the music. In the 30-second message, once you have decided what you want and who can give it to you, you then have to decide how best to get it. That's the *right approach.*

HOW TO FIND THE RIGHT APPROACH

Keeping in mind your obective and your listener, ask yourself these questions and answer them in single sentences:

> What am I talking about?
> What's the basis of my game plan?
> What's the heart of what I will say?
> What's the single best statement that will lead me to what I want?
> Can I comfortably build a case around this statement?
> What other vital statements will fit within or relate to this one?
> Will this relate to the needs and interests of my listener?

If the answer is the same to any two of those questions, and relates directly to your objective and the needs and interests of your listener, you have found the *right approach.*

Remember Richard Randall, our assistant bank manager who wanted a promotion to the job of manager? He did his homework. He had a lot of information about the executive who interviewed him. He knew what points he must address. The approach he chose to prepare for the interview was to emphasize his knowledge, experience, enthusiasm, and self-confidence.

The number of potential approaches to achieve an objective is unlimited. There are as many as your imagination will allow. But just as you should have only one clear-cut objective, so you must choose only one approach. Richard could have selected a different approach. For example, he could have told the executive that he wanted the manager's job because he needed more money to support his wife and kids. But Richard was smart enough to know that that approach had a poor chance of success because it didn't correspond to the executive's wants and needs. Richard chose the *right approach.*

OBJECTIVE AND APPROACH ARE ESSENTIAL TO EACH OTHER

There's a treasure in a sunken ship off the Spanish Main. Your objective is to get it, but you don't know how. What good is that objective without a plan, a way to get to the treasure? The way is your right approach. An objective without the right approach is useless.

You're leaving in the morning. You're either going by helicopter or you're going to ride a camel or you'll roller-skate, but you don't know where you're going. Ridiculous? Yes. But that's a perfect example of an approach without an objective. The right approach without an objective is useless.

The objective and the right approach are interdependent. Of course your objective will influence the approach you take to achieve it. Your knowledge of the needs and interests of your listener will also influence the approach you choose to take. But once you have settled on the right approach, it will serve you as a lifebelt or a parachute. A clear-cut right approach stated in a single sentence is a guarantee against ever forgetting what you're talking about. It's simple and direct, and always keeps you on track toward achieving your objective, no matter if you're talking to a single person or a roomful of people.

I get very excited about the power of having a clear-cut objective and choosing the right approach, and so will you the more you use them. They can be applied in every business and personal situation. Here are some examples:

Employee to boss
Objective:　to get a promotion
Approach:　A company must develop leaders to survive.

Dissatisfied customer to seller
Objective:　to get money back or an exchange
Approach:　I know good companies like yours stand behind their merchandise.

Employee to boss
Objective:　to get a raise
Approach:　I've proved the value of my work to the company.

Boss to employee
Objective: to keep employee without giving him a raise.
Approach: Everything in its time.

Customer to credit company or bank
Objective: not to pay incorrect charge
Approach: I'll be glad to pay when the charges are proven correct.

Salesman to customer
Objective: to sell diamond earrings to customer for wife's anniversary
Approach: What better way to show you love her?

One businesswoman to another
Objective: to get her to talk to a franchise dealer
Approach: Financial independence for women is wonderful, new, and exciting.

Customer to salesman
Objective: to get the best buy
Approach: I like your product, but I'm on a tight budget.

Nonsmoker to cigar smoker at the next table
Objective: to get him to stop smoking
Approach: I'm allergic to cigar smoke—it makes me ill.

Know *what* you want, know *who* can give it to you, and know *how* to get it: those are the essentials of every form of spoken or written communication. They are the *Three Basic Principles* of the most effective form of written or spoken communication—the 30-second message. And once you have those principles firmly in mind, you can put them all together in preparing your own 30-second message. Here's an example:

Ben Hollister, a manager in marketing, wants to take that two-week vacation he had to postpone six months ago. That is his objective. The marketing VP is the man who can okay the vacation. What is Ben's approach? This is what he said to his boss. Read it and see if you can find it.

"Do zombies make good managers? A vacation for me will pay off for you as well as for me. You know I work hard and love my job. I don't want to lose my enthusiasm, but I'm tired and I need to get away. I've got everything in good shape. If there's an emergency, Mary can handle it and I'll fill her in on any contingency.

"I'd like two weeks and I would appreciate going the first of next month. That will give me two and a half weeks to be sure everything is taken care of.

"When I come back I'll be able to work twice as hard and be twice as effective. Can I have your answer by Wednesday? Thanks."

Ben's approach was, "A vacation for me will pay off for you as well as for me." He chose the approach that would both fulfill his own objective and satisfy his boss's needs and interests. All in 30 seconds. That was the Yellow Brick Road to his vacation.

Of course, Ben just didn't march into his boss's office and rattle off his 30-second message like a prepared speech. But he had thought carefully about what he wanted to say, and after he introduced the subject of his vacation, he said it. If he had written a memo formally requesting a vacation, he would have said essentially the same thing. He had mastered the basics of the 30-second message. And so can you.

But a truly effective 30-second message contains something more than just three basic ingredients. As in a fine French stew that may be essentially a combination of meat, vegetables, and sauce, there are many other ingredients and flavorings that can be added to make it an appetizing dish. In the next chapter we will begin looking at the various extra ingredients that will make your 30-second message interesting, complete, and successful.

IN 30 SECONDS—OR LESS

The right approach is the single thought or sentence that will best lead to your objective.

The right appoach will also take into consideration the needs and interests of your listener.

The right approach will give you focus, and always keep you on track toward achieving your objective.

Knowing *what* you want, *who* can give it to you and *how* to get it are the *Three Basic Principles* of the 30-second message.

CHAPTER Five

The Hook

What allures, entices, tempts, tantalizes, fascinates, captivates, enchants, attracts, bewitches, catches, hypnotizes, makes you remember and gets you to buy a product, stay tuned to a show, or keep reading? A hook.

A *hook* is a statement or an object used specifically to get attention. Hooks are dangled in front of you every hour of the day and night as you watch television, listen to the radio, read newspapers, books, and magazines, and look at billboards.

Newspapers always use hooks. They're called headlines. A local paper ran a story about a husband-wife team that coaches women's track at a nearby college. The headline read, "FOR THIS COUPLE, LIFE'S A FIELD DAY." Here's a funny and creative hook from the staid *Wall Street Journal*. A front-page article about bat guano was headed: "BIRDS DO IT, BATS DO IT, BUT THE ISSUE IS WHO DOES IT BETTER?" And the subheading, a play on words: "PERUVIAN EXPORT FINDS U.S. IS FERTILE FIELD, BUT FIRMS HERE REFUSE TO CAVE IN," is a delight.

One of the most famous headlines of all time from the entertainment business newspaper *Variety* read: "HIX NIX STIX PIX." The story was about people who live in the country who don't like motion pictures about farm life. That headline got instant attention, sold out the issue, and kept the entertainment industry laughing and enchanted for years.

Television and radio use hooks too. They're called "teases."

"U.S. woman aviator picked up at sea by Russian sailors . . . a Romanian reporter here at the Olympic Games defects . . . and what do the police think about their own man who put the bomb on the Turkish truck and then reported it? All this and more on the eleven o'clock news."

You are allured and enticed into staying tuned.

Once a televsion adventure program begins, the first thing you see is action—shots fired, cars crashing, people falling off buildings. The producers take the most exciting parts of the show and stick them up front. You are hypnotized and captivated.

Television and radio commercials use hooks.

"It's not just growing a great potato that makes a great potato chip, it's how you slice it."

"The trouble with the average bargain trash bag is that what goes in doesn't always stay in."

You remember and buy the product.

Even books use hooks. The chapter titles of a book are a series of hooks to attract and fascinate the reader.

The first thing you must do when you talk to anyone —whether it's your employee, your associate, your boss, or the chairman of the board—is get his attention. You too must allure, entice, tempt, tantalize, fascinate, captivate, enchant, attract, bewitch, catch, hypnotize, and make them remember by using a hook at the start of your 30-second message.

FINDING YOUR HOOK

To find your hook for any 30-second message, answer the following questions:

- What's the most unusual part of your subject? Can you reduce it to one sentence?
- What's the most interesting and exciting part of your subject? Can you reduce it to one sentence?
- What's the most dramatic part? Can you reduce it to one sentence?
- What's the most humorous part? Can you reduce it to one sentence?

The sentences you come up with are the candidates for your hook. Now check them against the following questions:

- Does the hook lead to your objective?
- Does the hook relate to your listener?
- Does the hook relate to your approach?
- Will the hook excite or interest your listener?
- Can the hook be the first sentence in your 30-second message?

Whichever candidate best fulfills the requirements of these questions is your hook—almost.

Your last step is to determine if your hook serves better as a statement or a question. Test it by using it both ways. Either is acceptable, but I prefer a question when posible, because it's double-barreled. A hook is intended to get attention, and listeners usually pay attention when someone asks them a question. Which of these hooks would attract *your* attention?

"All good managers share one key ability."

"What one key ability do all good managers share?"

I prefer the second. And once you have decided between a statement and a question, you have your hook. But remember, whenever your hook is a question, it must be answered in your 30-second message. The answer to the question above is: "All good managers present themselves and their ideas effectively."

Arnold Brent, an executive, is talking with a group of his senior managers. His objective is long-range growth and prosperity for his company through continuity of good leadership. He knows some of his managers are consciously or unconsciously worried about training people who will someday replace them. But he also knows that every single manager is vitally concerned about getting his or her pension at the appropriate time. Brent's carefully planned approach is, "Developing qualified leaders means security for all of us." Here are two sentences. Which one of these should he use as his opening, his hook?

"We must develop qualified leaders."

"Do you really care who replaces you when you retire?"

If you picked the second you are right. The first sentence is a platitude. The hook becomes a turnoff instead of a turn-on and the message is lost. The second gets attention and draws the listener right into the whole message.

Here's how Brent made his hook work.

"Do you really care who replaces you when you retire? I do, because developing qualified leaders can mean greater security for all of us in terms of our pensions and the value of our stock after retirement."

Brent's hook related to his objective, his audience, and his approach. It was short, dramatic—and it worked.

USING HUMOR AS A HOOK

A hook can be serious, dramatic, or humorous, but it must capture interest. If it's dull, it won't accomplish its purpose, which is to get attention. Sometimes participants in my workshops feel they cannot start a serious message with a humorous or wildly dramatic hook. "But we're not in show business," they say. "Whether you like it or not, if you want to communicate effectively, you are," I answer. The more dynamic the hook, the more effective the total message becomes.

Humor, if used properly, is a powerful tool and a splendid hook. But I don't recommend using jokes unless your name is Bob Hope, and even then . . . There's too much chance of the joke falling on its face.

I speak from experiece. At the Beverly Hills Tennis Club, where I was having dinner, I overheard actor Walter Matthau tell a joke. Nobody laughed, but I thought it was great, so I stole it. Here it is:

Two cannibals were having dinner. One cannibal said to the other, "I hate my mother-in-law." The other cannibal said, "Just eat the noodles."

To make a point about how to get your listeners'

attention I tried the joke on all types of groups, from women executives to Chinese business leaders. The Chinese, who revere their mothers-in-law, laughed politely but without much conviction. The women executives, who were, or someday would be, mothers-in-law, didn't laugh at all.

You can never be sure of the reaction to a joke as a hook, so why take a chance? The best humorous hooks are anecdotes or personal experiences. And when you use them, you're not limited to one sentence.

For example, here's an anecdote I find useful to illustrate the topic of "learning all you can about your listener." Cary Grant's press agent said how tired he was of always being asked how old Cary Grant was. He had already been asked that same question twice the morning he received a telegram from a fan magazine editor, stating concisely, "How old Cary Grant?" He sent back an equally concise reply: "Old Cary Grant fine. How you?"

Here's another example. I was conducting a workshop at a Beverly Hills hotel, and there were six business executives in the large, elegant, and beautiful room. I asked each of them to come up with a hook, a simple statement that would get everyone's attention, and one young woman said, "A mouse just ran across the room."

"That's one of the best hooks I've ever heard," I said.

"And," said she, "it's also true."

It was. And that little mouse, I like to think, became one of the great communicators in the mouse world.

Humorous anecdotes and personal experience are excellent hooks, as long as they relate directly to your objective and your listener, and lead you to the point you wish to get across. Humor and the 30-second message that accompanies it make a hook memorable.

VISUAL HOOK

Sometimes the best hook is visual rather than verbal. In one of my communications skills workshops at a major American company, a presentation was given by five managers to senior management on "Fast-Tracking Minorities and Women." Two chairs were set in the middle of the room with an empty pair of women's shoes under each. The opening statement was, "Where are the people to fill those shoes?"

It was a specifically planned visual hook in conjunction with a terrific opening sentence. It worked wonders, and everyone at the company is still talking about it.

A professor at UCLA delivered one of the most brilliant hooks of all time. As he came out to talk about the architecture of great cities, he took a spectacular fall. He grinned and said, "Got your attention, didn't I?" That far you do not need to go. But if you do not engage your listener's or your reader's attention immediately, even a 30-second message will be lost.

HOOK AS EVERYTHING

You've learned that a hook can be a single sentence or a question. If you use an anecdote or personal experience as a hook, it can be a number of sentences. But a hook can also be the entire 30-second message, as long as it makes the point. A good example is the slogan of the San Diego Zoo: Extinction Is Forever. Three words encompass the objective (hidden), the approach, the hook, and the message. Here's another hook that says it all:

WHAT NOT TO DO IN BED

You can read.
You can rest.
You can sleep.
You can make phone calls.
You can eat breakfast.
You can watch television.
You can listen to music.
You can exercise.
You can snore.
You can even eat crackers—provided you're alone.
And, yes, you can snuggle.
But don't ever light up a cigarette when you're
    in bed.
Because if you doze off just once, all your dreams
    can go up in smoke.

R. J. REYNOLDS TOBACCO COMPANY

THE HOOK BOOK

Keep track of personal experiences and anecdotes that may make good hooks by jotting them down in a notebook. You can never tell when they will come in handy to help you get your point across in 30 seconds —or less.

Some time ago in Washington, D.C., I finished work around seven in the evening and I was tired. I thought a little exercise would help, so I walked to my hotel. On the way, I noticed some words carved in the side of the Veterans Administration building and wrote them down.

A year later I was writing, producing, and directing some television and radio spots for American Energy Week. I needed a hook. I opened my notebook, found these words, and wrote this spot for Charlton Heston to read:

> Carved in the living stone of the Veterans Administration building in the city of Washington are the words of Abraham Lincoln: "To care for him who shall have borne the battle and for his widow and his orphan."
>
> The men who died in our wars believed in freedom, the free and great country that we have. These days freedom and energy have become synonymous. March fifteenth through the twenty-first is American Energy Week. Seven days dedicated to a better understanding of the power that keeps us free.
>
> When you see a copy of the Declaration of Energy Independence to be given out American Energy Week, read it. Support it.

My hook book proved its value there, and yours will too.

IN 30 SECONDS—OR LESS

A hook is a statement or an object used specifically to get attention.

To get your listener's or reader's attention, use a hook as the first statement in your 30-second message.

Your hook should relate to your objective, your listener, and your approach.

Your hook can be a question or a statement, and it can be dramatic or humorous. If it's a question, it must be answered.

Anecdotes or personal experiences make excellent hooks.

Your entire message can be a hook.

Keep a hook book.

CHAPTER Six

Your Subject

It always pays to remember the three K's of communication:

Katch 'em.

Keep 'em.

Konvince 'em.

You katched 'em with the hook. Now you gotta keep 'em and konvince 'em.

The first thing a good trial lawyer does when preparing to address the jury is to build his case. He knows he must get the attention of the judge and jury. Therefore his hook. He also knows he must end with a plea on behalf of his client. Everything that comes in between is the *subject* of his presentation. The *subject* of your 30-second message must explain, reinforce, and prove the point you are there to make. In order to do this, the subject must contain all or any part of that famous formula: *what, who, where, when, why,* and *how.*

HOW TO DEVELOP YOUR SUBJECT

Step 1
Know your objective.
Know your listener.
Know your approach.

Step 2   Now ask yourself the following questions:
What am I talking about?
Who is involved?
Where is it?
When is it?
Why is it?
How do I do it?

Step 3   Check your answers against the following
questions:
Do they reinforce and/or explain my objective?
Do they relate to my listener?
Do they correspond to my approach?

If they fit the requirements in Step 3, any or all of
your answers to the five *what, who, where, when,
why,* and *how* questions are candidates for the subject
of your 30-second message. You can use them in any
combination or any order. Here's an example of a 30-
second message that uses all five.

An executive who is seeking investment in his company is talking with some potential investors. He sets
the hook.

"Can our stock double in value this year? I believe
it can and it will."

He then proceeds with his approach.

"We're in a fast-growth business."

Next he explains, reinforces, and proves his approach.

"Fiscal 1984 proved that again. It was the best year in our company's history—record revenues and record earnings. We now have a dominant and growing market share in the largest growth area in America. We're in the 'make you happy' business with a product to match that market. Our advance sales are already setting new records. Buy our stock now and participate. I did and I'm going to buy a lot more."

The executive told his listeners what he was talking about, where it was, when it was taking place, how it was progressing, and why they should buy.

Let's look at another 30-second message.

A doctor who is the medical advisor to a company is talking to one of its managers.

"How would you like to die young at a very old age? Preventive medicine is the answer. Did you know that a heart attack is just your heart getting angry with you? You can keep that from happening by treating your heart well and keeping it happy. All you have to do is exercise regularly, not smoke, avoid fatty foods, and give yourself a totally relaxed day at least once a week. Do these simple things and your heart won't get angry at you. I want you to stay healthy, so don't just come to me when you're sick. Call me tomorrow after I've had a chance to look at your test results. We can decide if you need to come back on Tuesday to discuss diet and exercise."

In this simple, concise, under-30-second message, the doctor knew his objective, his listener, and his approach. He told the executive what he was talking about—preventive medicine. Then he went on to tell him who is involved, and where, why, when, and how to stay healthy. He covered not just a few but all of the suggested ingredients that make up the subject of the 30-second message.

The subject is what any 30-second message is all about. It explains the point you want to make, answers the question you have asked in your hook, describes the job you want done. You may have chosen the right approach to achieve your objective, you may have captured your listener's attention with a provocative hook, but your message will be lost unless you *know* your subject, and present it as concisely and forcefully as possible.

Your subject is the news story that follows a dramatic headline, the caption under an eye-catching photograph, the candy in an attractive box. *What, who, where, when, why,* and *how* are all part of your subject. It's an easy formula to learn, and once you've mastered it, it will pay dividends in every 30-second message.

IN 30 SECONDS—OR LESS

The subject explains and reinforces your objective.

The subject relates to your listener.

The subject contains and corresponds to your approach.

What, who, where, when, why, and *how* are all part of your subject.

The subject is what your 30-second message is all about.

Know your subject and present it as concisely and forcefully as possible.

CHAPTER Seven

Ask for It

The Call to Arms, The Request, The Command, The Prescription, The Contract, The Bottom Line, The Close—they all add up to *ask for it!*

At the end of each 30-second message, you must ask for what you want.

A message without a specific request is a wasted opportunity. If you don't ask for something specific, the chances are you'll get nothing. It all comes down to one practicality: he who don't ask, don't get.

CLOSING YOUR MESSAGE

To determine the close that best fits with the objective of your 30-second message, simply ask yourself, "What do I want from my listener?" The answer to that question is your close. Next, think about the type of close that best fits the situation.

There are two types of close for a 30-second mes-

55

sage: a *demand for action* and a *demand for a reaction*.

DEMAND FOR ACTION

An *action close* demands a specific action on the part of your listener, and that action should not merely be implied. Here's an example:

A woman who was a member of the PTA told a group of her friends, "I'd like to set up an anti-smoking campaign at the school. Does anybody have any ideas?"

Everyone said, "Great, we'll think about it. Let's have some coffee and cake." Which they did, and that was the end of that. They got involved in other topics of conversation and the woman got no suggestions or help.

Here's the same situation with a strong action close:

"I'm worried about all the kids at school who smoke and I'd like to set up an anti-smoking campaign. This is important to me, and I'm sure to you, because it might help keep your kids from smoking, or help them quit if they do. Let's write down any ideas and suggestions you have while we're having coffee and cake."

That was a real situation. There were sixteen people present and the woman got sixteen responses. This example shows how valuable an action close can be. If you ask someone to perform a specific action within a specific time frame, you're more likely to get what you want.

This technique will work exactly the same way in a business situation. Here's an example:

It's the end of the day. You're having an informal meeting with four of your peers at the office to discuss ways to cut costs in your department. You can't tell your peers what to do, but you can ask them. If you say, "Gentlemen, we all know we have to cut costs. I've got a couple of ideas and you probably do too. Let's think about it," they'll say, "Sure, great, we'll think about it." And probably nothing will happen.

But if you say, "Gentlemen, we all know we have to cut costs. I'd really appreciate it if each of you would join me in writing down at least three ideas for accomplishing that and we can talk about them when we meet next Tuesday. It could mean a lot to all of us. Thanks for your help," you'll get results. Although you've asked in a polite way, you're really forcing them into a definite, specific action within a specific time frame.

DEMAND FOR A REACTION

We're all familiar with the hard-sell action closes of television commercials and sales pitches: "Buy now," "Come in today," "Take advantage of this once-in-a-lifetime offer." Equally familiar are soft-sell commercials that rely on the power of suggestion to get their point across. Instead of asking for a specific action, they demand a reaction.

There are often times when it may be impossible to demand a specific action—or it just may not be good strategy. That's the opportune moment for the soft sell or the *reaction close* which uses the power of suggestion or the power of example to get the desired results.

I was on the receiving end of just such a strategy when I saw a magnificent pair of seventeenth-century silver filigree candlesticks in an antique shop. They were for sale, but did the dealer say, "Buy them, Milo"? Never. He merely said, "Aren't they beautiful? You won't find a finer pair of candlesticks at that price. I don't know why no one has bought them, but I'm glad. As a matter of fact, I'm going to take them home tonight and keep them. My wife has been wanting me to ever since we found them."

Naturally, I couldn't wait to buy those candlesticks, and now when my wife and I look at them, I'm glad I did. I'm also a little wiser in the art of the reaction close.

CHOOSING YOUR CLOSE

Strategy is very important when it comes to choosing your close. The two operative rules are: *Know your objective* and *Know your listener*. It's important to weigh carefully how far you can push your listener. Sometimes an aggressive action close demanding an immediate response will get a *no* when patience and the power of suggestion of a reaction close might have gotten a *yes*.

Decide in advance what your strategy should be. But above all, don't walk into a blind alley. Always leave a way out. You won't get what you want if you don't ask for it. But if you don't know *how* to ask for it, you won't get it either.

IN 30 SECONDS—OR LESS

A message without a specific request is a wasted opportunity.

He who don't ask, don't get.

The *action close* calls for a specific action within a specific time frame.

The *reaction close* is the strategy to use when your best chance is to ask indirectly.

Decide your close in advance. Don't foreclose opportunity.

CHAPTER Eight

Paint a Picture

"Imagine yourself alone and starving. You're on a cement street surrounded by cement buildings. The buildings have no doors and no windows. The street is endless. There's no hope. That's what a lost or abandoned pet, a dog or a cat, faces when it's turned loose in the city."

Those words were spoken to me by a man from a charitable organization in Los Angeles called Delta. I got the message and couldn't wait to write him a check. I remembered some of the terrified animals I had seen in the streets and how my wife and I had tried to save them. He brought back those memories and moved me emotionally. He painted a picture I was unable to resist.

A truly effective 30-second message is more than a hook, a few words, and a close. Those words should paint a picture your listener will remember. They should be words your listener will understand. They should relate to your own and your listener's personal experiences. And they should reach your listener's heart.

Writers are familiar with these techniques. They're called imagery, clarity, personalizing, and emotional appeal. Any or all of the four can work independently or together for you in your 30-second message. Any or all can shape the hook, the close, a part of the message, or the whole message. Whatever the combination, they will give color and power to your 30-second message.

IMAGERY—COLORFUL PICTURES

When you communicate, you want your listener to "see" as well as hear what you're saying. Descriptive words help the listener visualize what you're talking about.

Look at these two sentences:

"Deficits will badly affect the economy."

"Deficits will spread a subtle, devastating poison through the economic bloodstream."

The first is dull, flat, without interest; it leaves no picture or image in your mind. The second paints a picture. You listen and assimilate what is said more easily because there's color to the sentence. And because you can visualize the words, you will remember the message.

Imagery is useful in all types of daily communication. Even on a recent plane flight, I watched it work. You know what the stewardess usually says when you land: "Please keep your seat belts fastened until the plane comes to a complete stop." These words go in one ear and out the other, but did I come to life when this stewardess painted a picture: "If you'd like to avoid the embarrassment of falling down in the aisle, please keep your seat belts fastened until we come to a complete stop."

It got a good laugh and the passengers stayed seated.

When preparing your 30-second message, think of descriptive words that help paint a picture for your listener. Words create images, and whether you're talking about a dog or a doughnut, you can make your message colorful, interesting, and memorable with imagery. In fact, using imagery in your 30-second message is one of the most enjoyable parts of the preparation because the very process forces you to be creative.

CLARITY

A major problem of communicating, particularly in the business world, is simply understanding what the other person is saying. People in different companies and industries often just don't speak the same language. They speak business-ese. Even within the same company, I've seen a lack of understanding because of the "language" problem.

A telephone company executive in one of my workshops prepared a 30-second message that included this sentence. "Specialized consumers duplicating terminal equipment add to operating costs." I was intrigued but puzzled. So I asked for a translation. What he meant was, "You're going to pay more money for your telephone service if non-phone companies duplicate existing equipment." That I could understand.

Many people seem to think it's necessary to use big words, technical terms, and complicated sentences to make themselves sound knowledgeable. In fact, just the opposite is true. Only someone who *truly* knows his subject can say what he wants to say in clear and simple language. The fastest way to put your listener to sleep is to talk to him in language he doesn't understand.

Here's the rest of the 30-second message that some telephone company executive prepared to use to explain an issue of concern to his customers, "bypass."

"Bypass refers to the use of telecommunications services, including microwave, radio, fiber optic systems, satellite, and cable television, to circumvent the local telephone company network. Industrial consumers bypassing the common carriers will deteriorate revenues and increase costs to residential consumers."

Here's the way the message sounded when he rewrote it for clarity:

"Think of your local telephone company as the Main Street Bridge, which costs $100,000 a year to operate, regardless of the amount of traffic. Cars pay one dollar and trucks two dollars to go across. A big company builds a new bridge just for trucks, and it costs one dollar a truck to go across. All the trucks use the new bridge. Main Street Bridge still costs $100,000 a year to operate. So now the cars, which paid one dollar, have to pay more because there are no trucks to help carry the costs. That is bypass. When big companies build their own telephone systems and bypass your local telephone company, you, the residential user, will have to pay more."

The telephone executive not only got his message across in 30 seconds in clear, understandable language, he also painted a picture that his listeners would remember.

There may be times when technical language is necessary. A computer salesperson had better know some of the language if he's going to convince a technically oriented buyer. But once again, the key factor to consider is your listener. You cannot achieve your objective if your listener doesn't know what you're talking about. Choosing words and images appropriate to your listener's level of understanding is the one surefire way of getting your point across.

PERSONALIZING

One of the simplest and most natural ways to get rid of business-ese in your 30-second message is to *personalize* by using a personal story to illustrate your point. If your listener can identify with you and a personal experience you have had, it will make your message much more effective.

An AT&T executive in one of my workshops was preparing a 30-second message to tell us why he felt AT&T was a better company than its competitors. The main point he was trying to get across was that when you dial zero, you get an AT&T operator. No other telephone company at that time furnished operators for the zero dial. "AT&T is a caring company," he said. "We want to serve our customers. We love to serve our customers. We furnish operators as a mark of the long service for which AT&T is justly proud," etc., etc.

Not only was the message boring, so was the speaker. He had no expression, no animation, no variety. He could have cured the worst case of insomnia in existence.

I asked him if he could personalize his subject. He did.

"Not long ago," he said, "my young son accidentally started a fire in our garage. I raced to the phone and dialed zero. I got an operator and within minutes the fire department was there and everything was under control. When I thought about it later, I realized for the first time how valuable and reassuring it is to know that in an emergency, I can dial zero and get an operator to help me. We're the only company that provides that service. Helping people—that's what AT&T is all about. Stay with us and keep it that way."

The AT&T executive personalized. Gone were the platitudes and the hype. We all identified with him and in less than 30 seconds, he communicated the message he wanted to get across. Moreover, the speaker himself changed as he delivered his message. He told his personal story with animation, expression, and true feeling—all of which made his message even more effective. He couldn't have done it better.

EMOTIONAL APPEAL— TOUCHING THE HEART

The most effective messages are those that reach the heart of the listener. Emotion causes change. If you can appeal to the emotions of your listener, he will become more receptive to your words.

Charities subsist on emotional appeals. How often have you written a check or made a donation because of a purely emotional appeal? Doing good for others makes you feel good about yourself. The same kind of an emotional appeal can work in your 30-second message. Here's a case in point.

Patricia Lewis wants to go into business. She's planning to open her own needlepoint shop. It means everything to her. She needs $10,000. She has $8,500. Where can she borrow $1,500? It's not a large amount, and Patricia knows she can always go to a bank. But arranging a bank loan takes time, and Patricia has found a good location and must move quickly.

She thinks about each of her friends. She has one, Jim Allen, a businessman with money to invest, but Patricia's small business wouldn't really be worth his while, even if it is successful. Then she remembers that Jim is a self-made man. He has talked often about the great opportunities this country offers and how he started out with nothing and made his dreams come true. That's it! Patricia decides to tell Jim that he could help make *her* dreams come true.

She makes an appointment to see Jim. They chat, and then Patricia gets to the point of her visit, her 30-second message.

"Jim, I have a dream. I want to open my own needlepoint shop. You know I have experience, and I'm willing to work hard. I've found a good location and I'm ready to invest $8,500 of my own money. But I need another $1,500. You probably remember someone who helped you make your dreams come true. I need your help to make *my* dream come true."

Patricia knew what she wanted, and who could give it to her. She looked for and found a way to reach him through an emotional appeal. Jim's heart was in the right place and Patricia got the loan. And you can easily do the same thing. You'll be surprised at how well it works.

IN 30 SECONDS—OR LESS

Imagery, clarity, personalizing, and emotional appeal will give power and memorability to your 30-second message.

Imagery: Think in pictures and use descriptive words your listener will remember.

Clarity: Use clear and simple language your listener will understand.

Personalizing: To illustrate your point, use personal stories that your listener can identify with.

Emotional appeal: Touch the heart of your listener. He will be more receptive to your 30-second message.

CHAPTER Nine

The Spotlight Is on You

Louis Armstrong sang a wonderful old song called "Whatcha Say" in a 1945 movie, *Pillow to Post*. The first line of that song is, "It ain't whatcha say, it's the way howcha say it."

It's undeniably true that *how* you say something is often more important than *what* you say. Now that you have mastered the three basic principles of the 30-second message and have become familiar with the other strategies and techniques that will help you get your point across, it's time to consider how to use this powerful new tool, and how you want to be perceived as you use it.

FIRST IMPRESSIONS

First impressions are often the most lasting. And if that first impression is not a good impression, you will have lost an opportunity that may never come again.

Last year, I had to have an operation for a torn cartilage in my knee. My internist sent me to see three surgeons, all expert in the operating procedure I needed. I had only a few minutes with each doctor, so how did I make my choice? My decision had to be based on first impressions. I picked the doctor I *liked* best, the one who impressed me the most. I was not buying the operation, I was buying the doctor.

How do most people choose the politicians they want to vote for? Candidates all say the same things on television, so most people vote for the ones they like, the ones they feel are most sincere and confident. They're not buying a politician's product, they're buying the politician.

If you're going to promote someone in your company, and it's a choice among three equally qualified people, you choose the one who has made the best impression on you. And you can bet the decision will be made the same way if you're one of the candidates for promotion.

Your overall image, your personal style, is the first impression you give. A concise 30-second message is your best guarantee of attracting and holding the attention of your listener. But that listener is also looking at you and forming an impression that may—or may not—help you get your point across.

Suppose you get a present—a gold pen. Would you rather be handed the pen, or would you prefer to receive it wrapped in an attractive box with a ribbon? Which is more exciting, more memorable, and more satisfying? The better you appear and the better you present your product—*you*—the more successful you will be.

STYLE AND IMAGE

Ralph Waldo Emerson wrote, "A man's style is his mind's voice." He was writing about individuality. He knew that how you look and act are nonverbal messages that speak volumes about the kind of person you are. We all convey a variety of nonverbal messages as we speak. We all look as we listen and make judgments accordingly. But it's a sad fact that most of us do not really know what we look like when we speak—and we are unaware of the impression we create on others. That's why the most careful preparation of your 30-second message is wasted if you don't pay equal attention to how you deliver that message. Here's an example:

A business executive in one of my workshops got up to deliver a 30-second message that he had polished to perfection. He knew his objective and his subject. He used a provocative hook. He asked for what he wanted. He even injected a little humor into his remarks. But as he spoke he just stood there, eyes cast down, unsmiling, his voice a monotone, delivering his 30-second message as if he had memorized it —which he had. The response from the other members of the group was somewhat less than enthusiastic. His nonverbal messages had overpowered his verbal one.

That performance led us to a typical workshop critique and discussion of the ways in which nonverbal messages are conveyed. We came up with the following list:

facial expressions, including eye contact
posture, gestures, and movements
tone of voice
physical appearance and clothing

All are part of your personal style. All can project a favorable—or an unfavorable—image. And please note that "the way howcha say it" applies to your entire conversation or presentation as well as to the vital 30 seconds.

SMILE

Among our many facial expressions, I think the smile is the most important. A smile inspires confidence and understanding. Nothing is more warming than a smile, when you mean it. And don't kid yourself: if you force a smile, your listener will know it's phony. To create a genuine smile, just think of something that amuses you. Better still, put some humor in your 30-second message. If you say something amusing with a smile, nine times out of ten your listener will smile right along with you.

People sometimes say to me, "But you can't smile in a serious discussion." And I reply that smiling in a serious discussion is not only good, it's mandatory. If everything you say is serious, there's no variety, no contrast. If your facial expression is blank, bland, or uniformly grave, there's no variety, no contrast. If all music were just one note, you wouldn't listen or care. The same is true if your words and facial expressions sound only one note.

71

Contrast is everything. Here's how smiling in a serious discussion provides contrast and makes the subject more dramatic. Read this sentence aloud:

"Many stories about children are amusing, but stories about battered children are frightening."

Now read it again. And this time, smile when you come to the words *are amusing*, then be serious for the rest of the sentence. Try it in front of a mirror. You'll see that a smile during the first part of the sentence makes the last part twice as dramatic.

A smile before you begin your 30-second message and after you conclude it creates a good first—and last—impression. It's a good way to introduce yourself to your listener—we all look more attractive when we smile—and a good way to thank him for his attention.

Eye contact also conveys important nonverbal messages. The speaker who stares off into space or keeps his eyes firmly glued to his shoelaces is not going to inspire much attention or confidence. In fact, he's revealing his own lack of self-confidence. In talking with a group, it's fairly easy to establish eye contact. Just keep your head up and vary the direction of your gaze. In a one-on-one situation, many people find it more difficult to look directly into the eyes of another person. And that other person may find it uncomfortable to be looked *at*. If you sense that in the other person, look straight at him anyway. Direct eye contact is an excellent way to emphasize a point and establish your own sincerity.

Your face is capable of expressing humor, surprise, puzzlement, concern—the full range of your emotions, any or all of which will add to the impact and meaning of your 30-second message. Variety of expression is the key to keeping your listener's attention and interest. No one likes to look at a blank wall —or an expressionless face—for very long. And remember, you may not be able to change the way you look, short of plastic surgery, but you can learn to vary your facial expressions and use them to good advantage.

EVERY LITTLE MOVEMENT

Your movements, gestures, and posture are just as revealing as your facial expressions. To prove that point, I recently tried an experiment in one of my workshops. After whispered instructions from me, a young woman spoke to our group, delivering an excellent 30-second message. Her face was animated, she established eye contact with the group, but as she spoke, she turned her wedding ring around and around on her finger. Not one member of the group could remember what she said. Their eyes, and their full attention, were riveted on that wedding ring.

I asked the young woman to deliver her message again, this time without any gestures or movements at all. She just stood there like a stick, but by this time, the group had caught on to what I was doing and began to laugh. No movement at all was just as distracting as meaningless movement. Finally, the young woman delivered her message for a third time. She seemed alert but relaxed and at ease. And when she gestured or moved, it was to emphasize her point. Her verbal language and her body language were working *together* to create an effective impression. The moral was clear to everyone: in the 30-second message, actions speak just as loudly as words.

Your posture—how you carry yourself whether you're standing or sitting—sends a double nonverbal message: it reveals what you think of yourself *and* what you think of your listener. If you slouch or shamble, it conveys indifference to how you look and to anyone who is looking at you. If you're rigid and uptight, you communicate anxiety and insecurity. Obviously, those are the two extremes, and I believe that in almost every situation you should try for the happy medium—relaxed but not *too* relaxed, alert but not tense—even when you may not really feel that way. Self-awareness is the secret. When you are aware of how you look to others, you can use that knowledge to look the way you *want* to look.

SPEAK UP

Not even the greatest pianist in the world can successfully play a concerto on a piano that is badly out of tune, or on a keyboard that has only one note. Your voice is *your* instrument. Its volume, its tone, its pitch, its expressiveness, and the skill with which you use it—all reveal your own state of mind and influence your listener's response to your 30-second message. If you deliver your message in a bored monotone, your listener will be bored. If your voice is shrill or you speak too rapidly, you're obviously uncomfortable and you'll make your listener uncomfortable too. Just like your facial expressions and body movements, anything about your voice that distracts your listener detracts from the effectiveness of your 30-second message.

The great actor Richard Burton used to amuse—and amaze—his audiences by reading the phone book and making it sound like Shakespeare. Abraham Lincoln, it is said, delivered the immortal words of the Gettysburg Address in a barely audible whisper. I don't recommend either. You're not making a speech, you're *talking* with your listener, and you should strive for all the qualities in your voice that make for good conversation: enthusiasm, variety, informality, and sincerity. If you believe in what you're saying, that will be reflected in your voice and your listener will believe it too.

WHAT TO WEAR

No one can deny that what you wear—and how you wear it—sends powerful signals. Apart from keeping us warm and dry and protecting our modesty, that's what clothing is for. Our clothing and accessories are an indication of our status, who we think we are and what we want others to think of us. The trouble is that sometimes that important message can be lost or misinterpreted; sometimes it's just plain inappropriate.

Talking about clothes with the business people— men and women—who attend my workshops, I find that our discussions usually revolve around two concerns: how to fit in and how to stand out. Or, what to wear to be one of the crowd without getting lost in the crowd. On the surface, that appears to be a contradictory question. But it isn't really. Not if you know who you are, where you are, who you want to be, and where you want to go. With that kind of self-awareness, you're halfway there.

Styles and fashions are always changing, and the first rule about clothes, accessories, and hairstyle is that there are *no* rules. It's up to you. If you're comfortable with yourself, then you'll be comfortable with whatever you wear. But trying to make yourself look younger or older than you are, or trying to look like someone you obviously are not, is the best way I know to make yourself and everyone else *un*comfortable.

It's always a good idea to avoid extremes, unless you're in the business of attracting attention to yourself. It's also a good idea not to be swept away by the latest fashion, even if a lot of other people are wearing the same thing. You should, of course, wear styles and colors that are becoming to you, that make you look your best. First, please yourself. But unless you live in a cave, you should recognize that, at some times and in some places and on some occasions, other people's opinions of the way you look and dress are just as important—maybe even more important—than your own personal preferences.

Speaking for myself, I'm never happier or more comfortable than when I'm dressed in a white shirt, white gabardine trousers with a colorful belt, and white shoes. But that's not the way I dress for business. I know the CEO of a major company who wears a baseball cap in the privacy of his own office, but not when he meets with his board of directors. A three-piece gray flannel suit is fine for New York, but it might be out of place in Houston or Singapore. You don't always want to look like everyone else. Use your imagination and do a little something to set yourself apart. You can be conservative and still wear a bright tie or handkerchief, a colorful blouse or shirt. But remember, your clothing is often the first thing people notice about you, and if you wear something that calls attention to itself rather than to you, then that may be *all* they notice. Your clothing and personal appearance speak for you before you've even said a word. It's only common sense to send the signals you want to send. All the rest is static.

In working with people in many different businesses and professions in many parts of the world, there's one thing about clothing and personal appearance that I always stress. In the long run, it doesn't really matter how expensive your wardrobe is, or how old-fashioned or up-to-date, as long as it gives the impression that you *care*. When you care enough to present yourself at your best, then people will care about you. If you're not really sure what makes you look your best, take the time and make the effort to find out, seeking advice from either friends or professionals. That, too, shows you care.

TRICKS OF THE TRADE

During one of my workshops in which I was speaking to a group of business managers about the importance of the nonverbal messages that go along with getting your point across in 30 seconds or less, one man said, "I thought I was here to learn how to communicate—not how to become an actor."

I wasn't offended. In fact, it gave me the opportunity to point out that communicating effectively *is* a form of acting. Every actor early in his career learns the importance of facial expressions and body movements. He learns how to use his voice and to "dress for the part." If he does not, there's no hope that he can create a character or communicate the playwright's message. And just as there are tricks to the acting trade, so there are tricks that you can learn to get your message across.

Your face

An actor rehearses his facial expressions as well as his lines. The hardest part for him is to *be* the character he is portraying and appear natural. Because the character you will play is yourself, you can't afford to have your facial expressions look forced or unnatural. Your goal is spontaneity and sincerity. Your goal is to be yourself. The best way to achieve this is:

> Be prepared.
> Don't memorize.
> Personalize.
> Care about what you are saying.

If you don't know what you look like when you're speaking, practice in front of a mirror. Knowing what your face looks like during your 30-second message will help you determine your effectiveness.

Body language

Using the body to depict an action or convey an emotion is what acting is all about. Charlie Chaplin, the great silent film star, created an unforgettable character and hilarious comic scenes without uttering a single line of dialogue. Your stage is much smaller, probably an office or a conference room, and again you're striving to be natural, not comic or dramatic. But will your 30-second message be most effective if you're sitting down or standing up? Whenever you have a choice, stand. It will always be more effective, because you can gesture and move more easily when emphasizing the point you're trying to make.

You cannot, as an actor can, see yourself in daily rushes or on rehearsal tape. But with a simple video setup, you can see the way you look to others. That's why I use videotape in all my workshops. It's always a startling experience to see yourself for the first time on that TV screen. "God, I look awful!" "Can that be me?" "Did I *really* do that?" These are just a few of the typical reactions. We all look and sound different than we think we do. But once you know how you do look and sound, you can go about making the necessary improvements.

Today video equipment is easily available to anyone at low cost. In my opinion, it's an unbeatable learning opportunity. I'll never forget "Sam," a participant in one of my workshops who asked if he could keep his videotape. "Milo," he said, "this workshop was incredibly valuable to me. I really learned something." Well, the training *is* good, I thought to myself, puffing up. "Tell me more," I said modestly. "What did you learn?" "I learned," Sam said, "after looking at myself on tape that I'd better lose fifty pounds."

Your voice

The voice is an actor's most important tool—and it can be yours too. Many people don't know how they look, and even more are unaware of how they sound. A few minutes speaking into a tape recorder and then playing back your voice can be a revelation. You will see immediately where it lacks color or variety, whether it's too loud or too soft. Do you articulate your words clearly? Do you give them the appropriate emphasis? If not, practice.

One of the best techniques for emphasizing an important sentence in your 30-second message is to speak the last few words softly. Let's try that technique with the following sentence. Say the first part in a normal tone of voice, then *almost whisper* the last two words.

IF I WISH TO EMPHASIZE SOMETHING, I . . . speak softly.

Using that technique, you can often see your listeners actually leaning forward to catch your words. You have captured their complete attention.

Another attention-getter is the pause. The pause is one of the most valuable speaking tools because it accomplishes so much. It gives emphasis to what you're saying. It gives you time to think. It gives your listener an opportunity to hear, absorb, and retain what you're saying. It also gives you a chance to see if your listener understands.

Obviously, you cannot pause 15 seconds in a 30-second message, but if you pause for one or two seconds at an important point, you'll find it adds a lot of drama to your message.

Read the following sentence aloud with a pause after the word *listener:*

> When I want to get the attention of my listener . . .
> I pause.

When you use this technique in your 30-second message, you'll see how closely your listener will pay attention during that short pause. He is intrigued to hear what you're going to say next.

Putting all these verbal and nonverbal techniques together in your 30-second message will make you an effective communicator. But remember, your goal is to be natural—to be yourself.

The rules are virtually the same for both the verbal and the nonverbal parts of your 30-second message. Know your objective, know your listener, and know your approach. Choose the words that will create the most favorable impression on your listener and help you achieve your objective. Then make sure the image you convey as you speak those words will help you achieve the same goal.

IN 30 SECONDS—OR LESS

First impressions may be the most lasting impressions. Make sure they are good impressions.

How you deliver your 30-second message is often more important than what you say.

If your facial expressions, especially your smile, are sincere and appropriate, they can make your 30-second message more effective.

Your movements, gestures, and posture should attract your listener's attention to your 30-second message, not distract it.

In delivering your 30-second message, strive for the qualities in your voice that make for good conversation—animation, enthusiasm, variety, informality, and sincerity.

Your clothes and personal appearance send powerful messages. Make sure they are the messages you want to send.

Be yourself.

CHAPTER Ten

One or a Thousand

How many times have you been desperate to escape some meeting as the speaker drones on endlessly? A short time ago, I was in Australia attending a dinner given for a major political figure. The gentleman spoke for approximately 45 minutes. He didn't really speak, though. He *read* his speech, barely raising his eyes from the paper. There was no rapport with his audience. Afterward no one remembered what he had said. It was a waste of time for the audience, a wasted opportunity for the speaker.

I'll never forget another occasion in Singapore when the speaker, who had already put a few of us to sleep, suddenly stopped speaking and, without a word, left the podium and walked right out of the room. We were mystified. Everyone was wide-awake now. What was he up to? What had happened? People began to talk to one another. Five minutes passed. Then, from in back of the hall, we all heard a noise, the sound of a flushing toilet. Conversation ceased as the speaker returned and continued his speech as if nothing had happened. I don't think he missed a sentence. And now he had his audience's complete attention.

30 SECONDS PLUS

Television by its intimacy has changed many of the rules of public speaking. The best speakers now are those who establish that same intimacy with an audience. They are natural and believable. They know that talking to a thousand people is essentially the same as talking to one person. The same basic techniques are used.

But if you know the natural attention span of any audience is about 30 seconds, how can you expect to capture and hold your listeners for two, three, five, or ten minutes? It's not that difficult if you think of your speech as an expanded 30-second message. Even before you begin to prepare your remarks, know your objective, know your listeners, know your approach. Consider ways to include the what, who, where, why, and when of your subject. Choose a provocative hook and an effective close. And as you work on your speech, use the clear language, the imagery, the personal anecdotes and experiences, and the emotional appeal that will best achieve your objective.

Once you have organized your speech as a whole, look at its parts. There will probably be more than one point you want to get across. Consider each of them as an individual 30-second message. During the two, three, five, or ten minutes that your speech lasts, you'll have an opportunity to ask—and answer—several provocative questions, paint more than one picture, use more than one personal anecdote or experience. The strategies that kept your listener alert and interested in your 30-second message will achieve the same effect in a longer speech. As a famous chef once told me when I asked him the difference between preparing an intimate dinner for two and a banquet for 500: "No difference. I use the same ingredients— just more of them."

MEMORIZING

Never memorize! You cannot communicate with your audience if you're struggling to remember each word of a speech. And what happens if you forget?

"Studio One" was one of the most popular shows in the golden days of live television. During one memorable broadcast, the scene was the interior of an airplane cabin. The plane was at an altitude of 30,000 feet, flying over the mountains of Tibet. Three men were in the cabin talking when suddenly there was silence. One of the actors had forgotten his lines. There were no retakes, no stopping of the action. That was it. Millions of eager viewers were glued to their black-and-white screens, waiting to see what would happen next. What did the actor do? He got to his feet, in an airplane cabin 30,000 feet over the mountains of Tibet, and voiced this immortal line: "Well, here's where I get off." He left the set and walked into history.

If *you* memorize a speech and forget it anywhere along the line, you'll have to get off that plane at

30,000 feet over Tibet—and there's no parachute. But even if you do find your way back, when you memorize, the material controls you, rather than you controlling the material. *Master* your material, but don't memorize. Memorizing robs you of being natural.

READING SPEECHES

Never read a speech to an audience! There is a big difference between the written word and the spoken word. They are different forms of expression. A well-planned, beautifully written speech may be powerful on paper, but when it's read aloud it can become stilted and unnatural.

So if you don't memorize or read your speech, what should you do?

PREPARING YOUR SPEECH

I believe you *should* write out your speech. But there's a special procedure you can follow that will guarantee that you'll deliver your remarks in the most natural way possible.

Outline your talk.

Use the same elements that you use in your 30-second message. The objective, the approach, the hook, and the close will all be the same. Only the subject will change. You will be able to develop it more fully.

Write your talk.

Following your outline, include all the facts and points you want to make—the what, who, where, why, when, and how of your subject—but *only* in rough draft form.

Reduce your talk to notes.

From your rough draft, write down key words on three-by-five cards that will remind you of what you're going to say. Set the card vertically when you write. You will then be able to hold the card less conspicuously in the palm of your hand when you give your speech. Larger pieces of paper would be cumbersome for you to handle, and a distraction to your audience. Your three-by-five notes will be a road map, leading you in the direction you want to go. And with notes instead of a written speech, you'll be able to deliver your remarks naturally, in your own words.

The following is a shortened version of a speech given by a representative of the telephone company as a public service to a mixed audience. First, you'll see the speech in outline form. Then, the speech itself as it was delivered from notes taken from a rough draft and written on cards.

Speech outline

OBJECTIVE: Get audience to recognize and use 911.
APPROACH: Dial 911 for your life.
SUBJECT: Brief discussion of 911 system.
HOOK: Who to call for help in emergency.

    I. Not one in a thousand knows emergency numbers.
       A. Dial 0.
       B. But over 80 emergency numbers. Valuable time lost.
   II. Better way.
       A. Assemblyman Charles Warren proposed 911 in state.
       B. In effect everywhere by 1986.
 III. Telephone companies working hard.
       A. Only in some parts of California.
       B. 911 will meet deadline.

CLOSE: Use 911. It might save *your* life.

Speech	**Notes**
Have you ever had a medical emergency in your house? What do you do? Who do you call for help? Do you know the numbers of your local hospital or ambulance service?	Medical emergency Who call?
Dial 911 for your life.	911 for life
Studies have shown that not one person in a thousand knows the emergency telephone numbers for fire, medical help, or law enforcement in their communities.	1 in 1000
In the past and at present, people with true emergencies generally dial 0 to call their local telephone operator, who looks up the right number and gives it to the caller or places the call for him.	Dial 0

But that takes valuable time, and in our area alone there are over 80 emergency numbers. So there must be a better way to cut down response time in emergency situations.	Time 80 emergency numbers
There is. 911. Assemblyman Charles Warren proposed 911 as a universal reporting telephone number for emergencies in the State of California. The bill was passed and all 911 systems are to be in and working by early 1986.	911 Charles Warren
	1986.
To meet that deadline, the California telephone companies have been working hard to provide the sophisticated equipment needed to put the 911 system into effect. But the system is very complex and expensive to initiate. That's why only some sections of California have access to it at this time.	Complex— expensive
We're lucky. Our area has the 911 service now. So the next time there's an emergency in your house, dial 911.	Dial 911
That's right. Dial 911. It may save *your* life.	Save your life

USING YOUR NOTES

Once you have made your notes, use them to rehearse your speech—as many times as necessary. Nothing is more distracting than a speaker who is unfamiliar with —or can't read—his own notes. You'll find that each time you rehearse from notes, your speech will be a little different—and better.

The use of notes during your speech is a tricky business. I saw a politician at a convention use notes to introduce his father. Imagine what *that* did for his credibility!

Never look at your notes when you begin a talk, at least not for the first two or three sentences. That's the time, above all others, when your remarks must appear to be spontaneous and unrehearsed. Can you imagine yourself meeting someone for the first time and referring to notes as you shake hands and begin your conversation?

During the course of your talk, use your notes only when necessary. Do *not* continue speaking as you look down at your notes. And when you look up again, pause briefly, then speak directly to your audience. When you finish your thought, keep looking at your audience briefly without speaking. This allows your point to set in the minds of your listeners. Talking into your notes destroys rapport, makes your voice go down in level, and weakens what you say. Whenever you speak, speak to your audience, not to your notes.

And one last point. When you come to the end of your talk, put your notes down and finish without looking at them. Never let your notes come between you and your audience.

YOU OR AN AUTOMATON?

Have you ever been in conversation with a speaker moments before he steps to the podium to begin his talk? There he is, chatting with you, smiling, animated, and friendly. Then as he begins his speech, everything human falls away and he becomes an automaton. That's because most people think they have to give formal speeches. *You're never there to give a speech. You're there to communicate with your audience.* And if you think of your audience, no matter how large, as one person you're chatting with in your living room, it will be easier to be yourself. Of course you'll be nervous. Even the most experienced speakers are nervous. But once you get into your talk, your nerves will disappear. You're well prepared and well organized. You've rehearsed. You have your notes. So don't be nervous about being nervous.

IMAGE AND STYLE

It will come as no surprise that your personal style and the image you convey during your speech are just as important as the impression you give during a 30-second message—perhaps even *more* important. The audience has more time to observe you and assimilate the impression you give. But on the plus side, you have more time to make sure that impression is a good one. You will usually deliver your speech in a more formal setting than your 30-second message. And instead of just one or a few listeners, you will have an audience. A speech really *is* a performance.

We've already talked about the nonverbal cues you give during a 30-second message with your facial expressions, your gestures and movements, the tone of your voice, and your personal appearance. The same basic rules apply when you're delivering a speech. Do nothing that will distract your audience's attention from your verbal message, or contradict it. And above all, be sincere and natural—be yourself.

In addition, here are a few more tricks of the trade that can pay dividends:

Even before you begin your speech, establish rapport with your audience by smiling and making eye contact. Look *at* your audience, not over their heads. Make everyone feel you're talking directly to him or her. And react to your audience's reactions. If you see their attention wandering, do something to bring them back.

Use gestures and movements to emphasize and reinforce the points in your speech, as long as they are natural. And in most cases, they will be natural when you personalize your speech and forget to worry about your gestures. Whenever anyone asks me, "What do I do with my arms?" I refer him to the centipede. Somebody asked a centipede which leg he started out with when he went for a walk. The centipede thought and thought about it—and was never able to walk again.

When you rehearse your speech, observe your gestures and movements. You can watch yourself in the mirror, ask friends or family to watch and comment, or best of all, watch yourself on video. Perhaps your company has its own video equipment. If not, you can rent equipment very reasonably.

Try to avoid using a podium or microphone, if at all possible. True, a podium is a convenient place to put your notes, but it also stands as a wall between you and your audience. And the voice that comes out of a loudspeaker in the far corner of a room may sound very little like *your* voice. Whenever you can, stand and talk directly to your audience, referring to notes concealed in the palm of your hand. You will feel freer and more relaxed, and so will your audience.

VARIETY

Variety is the spice of your speaking life. Without it, everything you say will be dull, boring, and ineffective. Also, you won't be very popular with your listeners.

By this time, you know forward and backward that the attention span of the individual is 30 seconds. Keep in mind that the attention span of an audience listening to a speech is also 30 seconds. That means if you wish to keep the interest and attention of your audience, you must do something different every 30 seconds.

You can smile, gesture, move forward, change your position, speak loudly, speak softly, speak rapidly, speak slowly, pause, ask a rhetorical question, be humorous, be dramatic, or be emotional. As with other techniques, putting variety into your words and movements may feel a little uncomfortable at first, but with practice it will become second nature.

CREDIBILITY

When you're speaking to a group, establishing your credibility is a top priority. You want your audience to know *why* they should listen to you, and a few brief words about your credentials will help your credibility. Better yet, tell a personal anecdote that will relate directly to your audience's experience and establish the fact that, even though you're the chairman of the board, a famous astrophysicist, or an expert in coronary bypass surgery, you're human.

Here's how a buyer for a company established his credibility with a large group of manufacturers. "Some years ago," he said, "I was offered a product at a price I thought wasn't quite as low as it ought to be. I didn't buy it for my company. Another company bought it and made a fortune. Was my face red! But I learned an important lesson. I learned that price isn't always the only consideration. That's one of the reasons my company has been fortunate to have seven top-selling items in a row in the last four years."

The buyer skillfully sold his successful abilities by telling a personal anecdote about one of his early failures. This technique can be called "making yourself human."

BEFORE YOU SPEAK

When you're invited to speak before a group, someone is always going to introduce you. Usually you're asked to send a résumé and someone in the group will put together an introduction from that. Or someone may call you just before the engagement and ask a few questions. Either way, all you can do is hope for the best.

There *is* a better way. There are two simple steps you can take to see that your introduction gets you off to a running start.

First, find out who's going to introduce you and, a day or so before your speech, give that person the necessary information for your introduction.

Second, and better yet, write your own introduction.

A friend and former client of mine was a top executive at Westinghouse Broadcasting whose job required him to introduce many guests on television. I asked him, "How would you feel if someone wrote his own introduction for you to give? Would that be presumptuous?"

"Not at all," he replied. "It would be great. It would save me time and effort, and he would be introduced just the way he wanted to be."

When you stop to think about it, an introduction, whether you're writing one for yourself or for someone else, is a 30-second message in its purest form. An introduction longer than 30 seconds is a speech. All the basic principles and strategies of the 30-second message apply to an introduction. The only difference is that a clever introduction should set up the hook the speaker wishes to use in his opening. Here's the way it works:

Nancy Adams, the president of a public relations firm, is speaking to a group of small-business owners on "How to Get Attention for Your Business." This is the introduction she wrote for herself:

"If you could choose anyone in this city to talk to you about how to get attention for your business, who would you choose? It's a good bet the name Nancy

Adams will be at the top of your list. Nancy began her career as the owner of a small business—a flower shop. Her flower shop became successful because Nancy recognized the importance of good public relations. Today, Nancy owns one of the best public relations firms in this city and numbers among her clients many small businesses as well as several major corporations. She still owns the flower shop where it all began. Here is Nancy Adams."

By writing her introduction this way, Nancy gave herself a lead-in to her opening remarks: "My clients and flowers have a lot in common. Both become more beautiful depending on how they are presented to the public . . ." She's off to a good start.

WHEN YOU'RE FINISHED

A well-known stage actor once told me, "You know, I never have much trouble playing a part. The real challenge is getting on stage—and then getting off." The same is true even with many experienced speakers. A well-written introduction with a good lead-in solves the first problem, but how many times have you listened to a speaker who just didn't know when, or how, to stop? Again, my advice comes from my experience with actors: "Always leave 'em wanting more."

No speech, in my opinion, should last more than ten or fifteen minutes. But however long, that speech should end *before* your audience wants it to end. That doesn't mean, of course, that you should trail off in mid-sentence, or fail to include some point you want to make. It does mean that, in preparing your speech, you should always have the first few—and the *last* few—sentences firmly in your mind. For variety and spontaneity, you can take as many liberties as you wish with what you say in between. But for me, making a speech is somewhat like telling a joke. The one thing you don't want to blow is your punch line. Knowing how you're going to end your speech will give you a target to aim at, a destination to work toward. And after you've hit that target and reached that destination, smile, thank your audience, and sit down.

IN 30 SECONDS—OR LESS

Whether your audience is one or a thousand, the same basic principles and strategies of the 30-second message still apply.

Don't memorize.

Don't read.

Outline your speech, write a rough draft, and then reduce it to notes on three-by-five cards.

Rehearse your speech, but strive for spontaneity, variety, and naturalness, in both your words and your movements.

Establish your credibility and describe your credentials in personal anecdotes.

Write your own introduction.

Know when to stop.

CHAPTER Eleven

Any Time, Any Place

In many business situations these days, a speaker will ask for questions after he has finished his speech. The 30-second message is the ideal means of handling question-and-answer sessions. It's the right size and shape to answer *any* question concisely. You can use it to reinforce points you have already made in your talk or to introduce and explain new points.

THE PERFECT ANSWER

A press conference is a good illustration of this technique in action. After a brief prepared statement, the person giving the conference asks for questions, and he gets them—often in bewildering variety. Some of them may relate to the prepared statement, asking for further comment and elaboration; others may come completely out of the blue. The secret of handling such a situation is careful preparation. The speaker has to anticipate and be prepared to answer any and all questions, but it would obviously be impossible to have every answer down pat. That's where the basic principles and strategies of the 30-second message come in. The skillful speaker previews in his mind the point he wants to get across in response to any anticipated question. His knowledge of his objective, his listener, his approach, and his subject allows him to frame an answer that is direct, concise, informal, and effective. In short, the perfect answer.

My associate and I recently conducted a training workshop for senior representatives from Scotland Yard and the Northwest Mounties, chiefs of police from some of our major cities, and FBI agents. All were marvelous at asking questions, but not so good at answering them. In fact, many were inclined to take a "no comment" and a low-profile position, which, they had come to realize, merely intensified curiosity and invited more questions.

At the workshop they learned a new strategy for handling even the most difficult questions. They learned that, first and foremost, answering a question gives *you* the opportunity to talk. You must answer the question as concisely and truthfully as possible, but then you can use that opportunity to get your own point across. Here's an example I used in my workshop:

After a series of crimes in a city park, the aroused citizens of the neighborhood were demanding action. A police captain agreed to answer their questions, and one man asked angrily why no arrests had yet been made. "Even though we have very little evidence to go on," the police captain said, "we're pursuing every lead. We have also stepped up police patrols of the area and the lighting is being improved. Your park is much safer now." The police captain answered the question, and while that answer may not have been the one the angry citizens wanted to hear, he took the opportunity to reassure his audience and get his own point across.

Once those law enforcement people utilized this technique, their philosophy changed. Instead of avoiding interviews, they looked forward to them. This same strategy will enable you to get your point across during any question-and-answer situation, whether it's in a talk to a business organization, a meeting with office associates, or a tax audit by the IRS.

THE QUESTION TURNABOUT

You can also use the same strategy in a one-on-one business situation. The opportunity to get your point across is almost always there. If not, you can create your own opportunity. Here's the way it works:

John Conway, an assistant director of human resources, is preparing for an upcoming meeting between employees and the union. The issues at stake are technical and difficult and he wants to hire a consultant. His boss must okay the proposal, but he's a busy man and John knows he must be concise. He carefully prepares his 30-second message and waits for the right moment to present it.

If, during one of their periodic meetings, John's

boss asks him directly about the upcoming meetings, John is ready with his proposal. But what if John's boss doesn't ask the right question? There's a strategy for handling that too.

In the same situation, John's boss might say, "By the way, how are you progressing on the medical insurance report?" John's answer: "It'll be on your desk next Tuesday. As well as a list of the important topics we'll be discussing at the next meeting with the union. Incidentally, there are some vital issues to be decided. I think we could use expert advice and I suggest we hire a consultant. . . ." Note that John answered the original question, but then skillfully used it to flow into the point he wanted to make.

There's always a way to answer a question and turn it to the point you wish to make. The trick is in the transition. Here are some transition phrases to take you from the answer you give to your prepared 30-second message:

"I don't know about that, but let me tell you about . . ."

"You're absolutely right, and one other point is . . ."

"I'm sure that's true, and another thing I'm sure of is . . ."

"That can wait until tomorrow, but something that can't wait is . . ."

"I agree with you, and I'm sure you'll agree that . . ."

You'll find that with almost no practice the transitions will become easy, even though at first they may seem contrived to you. But there's nothing devious or dishonest about this technique. You're making a point clearly and concisely, a point that you have come there to make. And that's what communicating is all about.

ON THE PHONE

Humphrey Bogart, in the years shortly before he died, refused to do television, as did many stars of those days. As head of talent and casting at CBS Television, I wanted Bogart. But Sam Jaffe, the agent who started his career and still represented him, said, "Forget it, Milo. He won't do television under any circumstances."

I knew there had to be a way, and finally I came up with an idea. The part of Duke Mantee in a play called *The Petrified Forest* had catapulted Bogart to stardom. Then came the film, which established his movie career. I talked with the powers that be at the network. I told them we "just might" get Bogart if we did *The Petrified Forest* as a television special.

They said, "Okay, we'll do it. But *only* if you can get Bogart."

Sam Jaffe gave me permission to call Bogart. I knew Bogart treasured his time. If I couldn't get my point across in the first 30 seconds, I'd lose him. I planned and prepared my 30-second message.

I got Bogart on the phone. After identifying myself, I said, "What's the most exciting, important, and rewarding project you've done in your whole career, Mr. Bogart?" I had his attention. "It was *The Petrified Forest*, wasn't it?"

I could hear the enthusiasm in his voice when he replied, "It sure was."

"We're planning to do the play here at CBS as a television special," I said. "It'll be a major project. We'll give it all the care and quality it deserves. Still, we know it won't be the same without you." I paused and I could almost hear Bogart thinking, "They want me, but they're going to do it anyway." I knew, or hoped, that thought would get him. He couldn't stand to have someone else play the part he had made famous. I didn't dare tell him if he said no, we wouldn't do the play. Then he'd be off the hook. "We desperately want you as Duke Mantee," I continued. "Will you do it?" I really was holding my breath.

"Milo," he said, "you know I don't do television. Not yet."

"Mr. Bogart," I said, "with you in the part, this show will be what it ought to be. We'll be proud of it and so will you."

There was a long pause at the other end of the line, then Bogart said, "You know my weak spot, don't you? I'll do it."

There's no limit to the usefulness of the 30-second message, and the telephone is one of the best places to put it into practice.

Business people are, by definition, busy. Often they don't have time to take or return telephone calls, especially when they know the caller takes forever to get to the point. Getting your point across in 30 seconds can change all that. When your business contacts learn you're always concise, they'll speak to you or return your calls promptly. You'll get results—and save money on your phone bill.

We've all received telephone solicitations. You don't know the caller and the caller doesn't know you. In fact, your number may have been dialed by a computer. And the caller knows he has even *less* than 30 seconds to attract and hold your attention and get his point across. Otherwise, you'll hang up. You can bet he has his message carefully prepared.

You should be just as carefully prepared whenever you make a business call, whether it's to sell a product or a service, ask for an interview, arrange a meeting, ask for information, or register a complaint. Know your objective, your listener, and your approach *before* you make the call. Capture his attention with a provocative hook, explain your subject concisely, and then ask for what you want. A telephone call is meant to save time, and an effective 30-second message is the best way to ensure that you won't waste your listener's time—or your own. It worked for me with Humphrey Bogart. It can work for you too.

But what if you can't reach the person you want to talk to? A secretary or an assistant says, "I'm sorry, he's in a meeting (on the other phone, out of the office) at the moment. Do you care to leave a message?" *Of course* you care to leave a message, but it should be the *right* message. It won't be the full 30-second message you've prepared. But it should include the reason why you called, and a *good* reason why your call should be returned—all in a couple of sentences the secretary can jot down and present to the boss, along with your name and number. If your name is unfamiliar, nine times out of ten your call won't be returned unless the person you're trying to reach knows what you want and how it will be of benefit to him.

ANSWERING MACHINES

Still on the subject of telephones, answering machines have become a fact of life these days. But how many times have you dialed a number and heard something like this: "Hello, this is the Fry residence. Unfortunately we are not home at the moment, but we will return shortly. This is our answering machine. Please leave your name and phone number, the time of your call, and any message you may have after you hear the sound of the beep. We will return your call as soon as possible. But please remember, do not speak until after you hear the beep. Thank you."

Beep.

I know when I call the Frys, I waste more time listening to their message than it would take me to give them mine. So I don't call unless I have to.

I've also heard everything from music and jokes to a professionally recorded message on an answering machine that made me wonder who I was calling. Although an answering machine does give you an opportunity to have fun, the simpler your message is, the easier it is for the caller to leave his own message.

Nobody really likes talking to a machine. In fact, some people are so nervous about telephone answering machines, they freeze and don't know what to say. A standard 30-second message for answering machines can solve that problem. It's really very simple. If you're nervous about being recorded, simply keep the message next to the phone and read it when an machine answers your call. Here's a sam-

his is (*your name*). I'm calling about (*what
ing about*). Sorry I missed you. Please call
me at your convenience. I can be reached today at
(*your phone number*). Thank you.

Even if you reach a real person at an answering
service instead of a machine, always be sure to leave
your number. That will save the person you're calling
from having to look it up and your call may be returned sooner. And again, if the person you're calling
doesn't know you, give him or her a good reason to
call you back.

THE 30-SECOND SALES PITCH

It's a very good salesman indeed who can make a successful pitch over the phone. On most occasions, the
phone call merely paves the way for an appointment
or an interview. The sales pitch is made in person,
and all the basic rules and techniques of the 30-sec-
ond message, both verbal and nonverbal, couldn't be
put to better use. The good salesman knows his objective, his listener, and his approach *before* he begins
his pitch. He knows his product or service and knows
why it would be of benefit to his potential customer
or client. He asks for what he wants, even if it's only
another appointment when there may be time to explain more fully what he has to sell. Here's an example:

Doug, an air-conditioning company representative,

drops by the purchasing department of a potential commercial customer. He knows the head of purchasing, Mr. Loomis. Although Mr. Loomis is harried and busy, he takes a moment to see Doug. But as they exchange pleasantries, Doug realizes this is the wrong time to try to make a sale. He feels that if he can get a specific appointment the next day, he will have a much better opportunity. He quickly gets to his 30-second message.

"Mr. Loomis, does the temperature of your building interior really make a difference? You know it does. Studies prove that people are more productive within a certain temperature range—happier too. Our new equipment will pay for itself and make you money as well. And it has two features that are different from any other air-conditioning equipment. May I please come in tomorrow and demonstrate our new system for you?"

The salesman intrigued the purchasing head. He was concise and to the point. He got his appointment —and made the sale.

Most discussions between salesman and customer, however, usually take a lot longer than 30 seconds. They may include meetings with other associates, sometimes even drinks or dinner. But whatever the time span, whatever the business or social situation, the 30-second message, delivered at the right moment, is still your best weapon to get your point across and make it stick. And it never hurts to repeat that message as many times as necessary, as long as you rephrase it or elaborate upon it in slightly different ways every time. Repetition is a standard technique in advertising. Ads drum a slogan or name of the product into the potential buyer's mind. You may want to achieve the same objective, but with all of the many techniques and strategies of the 30-second message, you have a variety of ways to get your point across. And last but not least, making a sale is almost always a two-way conversation. Once you've presented your point, you can expect your potential customer to ask questions. Here again, a concise 30-second message is the best way to answer those questions and make additional points of your own.

MEETINGS

I've never talked to anyone in any company who didn't think that meetings were too long, too frequent, and too boring. They don't have to be. Business meetings are often inconclusive and boring because the participants are not well prepared. There is too much ground to cover, too many ideas and subjects to be discussed, too many choices to be made. You must narrow them down *before* the meeting so key points can be properly examined and logical decisions arrived at. The meeting should have a specific agenda, and it's up to the person who is calling and conducting the meeting to prepare it.

The basic principles of the 30-second message can be used to prepare an agenda. First of all, state the *objective* of the meeting—what it is you hope to accomplish. Second, state the *approach*—the way or ways in which it will be possible to achieve your objective. Then state the *subject* or *subjects* that will come under discussion. And finally, ask for what you want, in this case for every participant to address each key requirement of the meeting with a 30-second message stating his opinions or recommendations. Such an agenda will force careful consideration and preparation. It may mean more homework, but the result in the long run will be a substantial saving of time and money.

Here's a sample agenda:

> OBJECTIVE: to improve our cash position
> APPROACH: to sell or not to sell the uptown facility
> SUBJECTS TO BE DISCUSSED:
> 1. Uptown facility only marginally profitable, but there are prospects for improvement.
> 2. Buyer available now but at a depressed price.
> 3. Sell now or wait and hope for increased profits and/or better price.
>
> Please be prepared with a 30-second statement of your opinions and recommendation. The meeting will begin at 2:30 sharp and will finish no later than 3:00.

There are some meetings, of course, where the subjects under discussion are much broader, where informality is the keynote, and where the give-and-take of everyday conversation is both required and beneficial. Even so, when it's your turn to speak or to answer a question, make your key points in 30 seconds or less. Your associates not only will be impressed, they will be grateful.

IN ELEVATORS, RESTAURANTS, AND OTHER PLACES

The typical Horatio Alger tale revolves around that lucky moment when the poor boy rescues the millionaire, is rewarded with a job, works hard, marries the millionaire's daughter, and ends up a millionaire himself. Luck often plays a part in business communications. You might, for example, run into the very man you've been trying to see for weeks in the elevator, or at a club or restaurant. You could, in fact, make your own luck and engineer such a meeting. But most often it just happens. And when it happens, you should be prepared. The 30-second message is your ammunition. You know what you want, and there's the man who can give it to you. But you also have to know how to aim—and when to hold your fire.

Jack Marshall and his wife are having dinner in a restaurant with a group of people from his company, including the president and his wife. Jack has an idea he knows the president will be interested in. Is this the time and place to speak to him? Jack decides to try, but there are careful judgments to be made. First, he must choose the right moment. He must wait until the president, Mr. Caldwell, brings up the subject of business. If Mr. Caldwell asks how things are going in his department, Jack will have his golden opportunity. And that's just what Mr. Caldwell does. Now Jack has the president's undivided attention—but for how long? If he fumbles around or is unclear in his objective, his opportunity will be wasted and the president will probably think less of him. But if, without pressuring or putting the president on the spot, he can get across his *prepared* 30-second message, he may change his whole future. Jack makes his move.

"Everything is going fine, sir. In fact, I've just been testing a new procedure to speed up deliveries. The tests have proved conclusively that it works. We'll save time and money. I'd like to talk to you about it. May I call your secretary and make an appointment?" The president smiles and nods affirmatively.

In this situation, Jack both created his own opportunity and took advantage of the opportunity the president offered him. He made the right judgments—and he was prepared. He got the appointment, and a promotion when his new procedure was adopted by the company.

TOASTS

Many toasts are made on the spur of the moment. But if it's an important occasion, you should plan your toast in advance.

A friend who is a major political appointee to another country told me she was going to make a toast to a gentleman who was very special in her life. The occasion was a huge birthday reception in his country —the country of her assignment. She wanted the toast to be perfect. She followed these simple and familiar rules. No toast should last more than 30 seconds, and you can prepare your toast just like any other 30-second message. Know your objective, your listeners, and your approach. Find a hook, and follow it with your subject and your close.

Here's what my friend said at the birthday reception:

"I was a stranger in a strange land. I came here to serve my country. My country has served me. I have found warmth, understanding, beauty, and love. Now I am no longer a stranger and I would like to thank the man who made it possible. What better time than on his birthday, and what better way than with love and honor? To Jim."

Even in sad situations, or sometimes especially in sad situations, humor can do wonders in a toast.

An old friend of ours had died. He was one of the greatest motion picture agents in the history of Hollywood. Clark Gable, Wallace Beery, and Fred MacMurray were just a few of the clients whose careers he guided. He had also been a lover of the good life, elegant restaurants, good food, and great art. He always wanted and got the best of everything.

The small group of friends gathered in his home were feeling sad and solemn. But his wife, knowing he wouldn't have wanted us to be unhappy, stood up, raised her glass, and said a few words I'll never forget:

"Here's to Phil. Wherever he is, he's at the best table."

A toast is, as a rule, an emotional message. But be of good cheer, because you don't have to be stylish or witty. Feeling and sincerity are what matter. Whether you have planned ahead or get a sudden, on-the-scene urge, the single most important rule for an effective toast is to say exactly how you feel with all your heart.

30 SECONDS ON PAPER

Attention span doesn't change for the written word. It's still 30 seconds. The hand is quicker than the eye, but the eye is quicker than the mouth. That means you can read more words on paper in 30 seconds than you can speak aloud in the same length of time. The difference doesn't matter. What does matter is that you should present no more on paper than can be read in 30 seconds, or you'll lose the dynamic effect on your reader.

How many times have you received letters of several pages asking for your business or for a charitable donation? How many times have you thrown them in the wastebasket even before you finished the first paragraph? To get your point across effectively in a letter, all of the principles and strategies of the verbal 30-second message should be used. Know your objective, your reader, and your approach. Begin your letter with a hook, develop your subject concisely, and end with a powerful close. And there's one other rule: keep it to one page. If there are any technical explanations required, include them on separate paper to be read *after* you have got your reader's interest and attention with your one-page letter.

Here's a letter designed as a follow-up to a middle-management training program.

> Dear Bill:
> Did the result justify the money?
> The training program just completed in New York
> with Ralph Johns and his people was even better

and more valuable than I had anticipated. I suggest all five of our general managers participate in the program.

Our objective
to increase company profits
Our approach
to better prepare our managers to understand the operation of the company and sell its products
Subjects
1. familiarizing our managers with the functions and responsibilities of every department
2. planning and coordinating ways to ensure close cooperation among departments
3. exploring new markets and marketing techniques to sell our products

If you haven't spoken to Ralph Johns, please do so. I think he will tell you that the benefits of the training program have already more than justified the expense. If you agree, I will appreciate your help in continuing this program for our company.

Please call me.

Sincerely,

The message, even though detailed, is on one page. It can be read through in 30 seconds. It holds the reader's attention. That's why it's important to be brief, concise, and well organized.

MEMOS

A memo is an abbreviated letter. And a memo is something to jog the memory. The shorter the better.

To all employees:
Closed for the holiday next Friday, June 12th.
Enjoy.
The Management

That memo said everything it needed to say, didn't it?

There are formal and informal memos, but it is well to remember that a business memo should conform in every regard to a spoken 30-second message. Here's an example:

September 30, 1986

TO: _____

An Accounting Department meeting is called:

DATE: Wed., Oct. 9, 1986
TIME: Commence 8 A.M.
　　　　Conclude 9 A.M.
OBJECTIVE: to save time and money
APPROACH: reorganization of the Accounting
　　　　　　　Department
KEY POINTS: These are included in the accompanying materials, along with cost breakdowns of new equipment and procedures.

Please read and study all enclosures. If you have questions, call Oscar Peterson (ext. 906) so you will be well prepared for the meeting.

We will expect and appreciate a concise recommendation from each of you on the salient points contained in the enclosures.

　　　　　　　　Thank you,
　　　　　　　　J. Y. Donahue
　　　　　　　　Chief Financial Officer

In preparing this memo, the chief financial officer knew what he wanted to achieve. And its readers will know exactly what is expected of them.

LETTERS OF RECOMMENDATION

Letters of recommedation or introduction are another form of the 30-second message and should be no longer than one page. Here's one for Lyle Riorden, a public relations director, written by the president of the company for which he used to work.

> Dear Mr. Anderson:
> Lyle Riorden has disproved the old adage: "You can't teach an old dog new tricks." As the public relations director of our company for the last seven years, Lyle taught a lot of us "old dogs" new tricks, including a more thorough understanding of the importance of public relations. It's not an exaggeration to say that Lyle put our company on the map.
> We were sorry to lose Lyle when he moved to your city. But he did a splendid job here and I believe he would be an asset to your company.
> Please feel free to contact me for any additional information about Lyle that I might be able to give.
> Sincerely,

THANK-YOU NOTES

A thank-you letter or note is a thoughtful gesture, and it's also good business. Keep your thank-you notes short, sweet, and sincere.

116

Dear Bob,
My new boss tells me that you recommended me
highly when he called you. I don't know what you
said, but it worked. I got the job. Many thanks.

Cordially,
Jennifer

Thank-you notes are often forgotten in the business
world. A thanks in person or over the phone is equally
effective, but if someone has gone out of his way to do
a good job or a favor for you, it's worth a few minutes
of your time to write a note to let him know you're
grateful. It doesn't have to be long. It just has to be
sent.

IN 30 SECONDS—OR LESS

A concise, 30-second message is the perfect answer to
any question.

Using the question turnabout, you can get your own
point across in answer to any question.

Know your objective, your listener, and your approach *before* you make any business phone call.

If you can't reach the person you're calling, leave a
message giving him a good reason to call back.

Make all the key points in your sales pitch in 30
seconds—or less.

A carefully prepared agenda, calling for concise, 30-
second statements from participants on all key points,
will save time in any business meeting.

You can take any opportunity to deliver your 30-

second message. You can even make your own opportunity, if you are prepared.

All the rules and strategies of the 30-second message can be applied to your written business communications.

Written or spoken, the 30-second message is the most effective way to get your point across. Use it.

CHAPTER Twelve

The Ultimate 30-Second Message

My friend Charlie was in love with a charming young woman named Ava. She was in love with Charlie, but so far he had been unable to persuade her to marry him. Then one day he invited her to lunch. They drove to the Los Angeles Coliseum, the largest sports arena on the West Coast, the home of the classic UCLA-USC football games and the site of the Olympic Games of 1984.

In the center of the vast playing field were placed a small table and two chairs. A maître d' showed them to the table, a captain seated them, and a waiter waited behind each chair. Apart from this small oasis, the Coliseum was empty. Thousands of empty seats stared down at Charlie and Ava.

The table was elegantly set with Spode, crystal, and silver. Caviar and champagne were served. No Coliseum hot dogs here. Then a soufflé and salad with more champagne. And as they were waiting for des-

119

sert, Charlie directed Ava's attention to the huge electronic scoreboard at the far end of the field.

In a prearranged signal he raised his glass, and on the board flashed the words, "Darling Ava, will you marry me?"

She said yes, and Charlie and Ava are living happily ever after right here in Los Angeles.

Of course, Charlie's message took quite a bit of advance preparation. But he got his point across in 30 seconds—or less.

And now that you know how it's done, so can you.

You're ready.

Go out and do it.

ABOUT THE AUTHOR

MILO OGDEN FRANK is a nationally acclaimed authority on communications skills and strategies. His proven techniques have brought him success in an extraordinary career as an actors' agent, Director of Talent and Casting for CBS Television, a writer-producer of feature films at MGM and independently, vice president in charge of production for Cinerama. He is also a many-yeared veteran of communications skills seminars for business and politicians, a lecturer, and the only American working in his particular area with Chinese, Japanese, Indians, and Malaysians in Southeast Asia. Mr. Frank and his wife live in Beverly Hills, California.